MYSTERIES CARVED IN STONES

Stories Beneath the Ancient Relics

Rup Rani

LiliumWind Publication

CONTENTS

PREFACE

Hello there, fellow explorer of the past, and also welcome to the exciting world of "Mysteries Carved in Stones."

Prepare yourself to go on a journey through time, a journey that will expose the mysteries as well as wonders of ancient discoveries that have been concealed for a long time. This non-fictional trip, guarantees to be a tapestry of intrigue, a gold mine of details, as well as an invite to sign up with the ranks of history's most adventurous travellers.

As we make our method with the phases of this publication, we will begin on a journey to resolve the secrets surrounding the artefacts that have stood up to the attack of time. These artefacts, which can be found all over the globe, are greater than simply relics of lost ages; instead, they are doorways to worlds that took place a very lengthy time ago as well as gateways to tricks that we have not yet been able to completely comprehend.

You may be wondering why there is yet one more publication on old artefacts. Because " Mysteries Carved in Stones" is not simply a retelling of historic artefacts; instead, it is a monolith of the voracious curiosity of people, an examination of the impervious troubles that tantalise our intellects, as well as a celebration of the marvels that have enthralled centuries of people.

The method in which we handle these artefacts is just one of the important things that makes this book unique from others. We are not below to just recount occasions or supply a sequential order. Instead, we are going on an expedition that will certainly dive deeply into the enigma bordering these artefacts by checking out the unwritten stories, the misconceptions, and also the quandaries that are connected with them. These antiques are not non-living items but instead containers that are loaded with the echoes of old voices; it is time for us to pay attention to what they have to state.

These pages will certainly direct you via the process of analyzing the keys of the Nazca Lines, which are etchings that stumble upon the completely dry landscape of Peru as well as can just be seen from above. We will discuss the possible definitions of these huge geoglyphs, which have been analyzed by a selection of means, ranging from huge schedules to unusual transmissions of information.

Our journeys will likewise take us to Easter Island, residence to the mysterious Moai, which are huge stone figures that stand guard along the island's coastline. That carved them, as well as for what usage were they sculpted? Rup Rani will certainly serve as our navigator as we make our means through the labyrinth of background, and stories, as well as proceeding research in mission of response to the Moai's timeless enigma.

We are most likely to consider the mysterious Voynich Manuscript, which is an old publication that is packed with text that can not be analyzed and unusual pictures that have puzzled academics for decades. Is it a well-crafted scam or may it be the means whereby long-forgotten info may be uncovered?

We will certainly go throughout the world as well as through the ages to find the stories that exist behind these relics and the secrets that they maintain. Our journey will start in old Egypt as well as finish with the strange codices of the Mayan people. You will find that you are fascinated by stories that are loaded with exploration, enjoyment, as well as marvel.

My words expand an invitation to travel back in time, to perch on the edge of knowledge, as well as to take an appearance right into the unidentified. I have performed extensive research on these prizes, bringing up not just realities but also anecdotes that will certainly pique your interest and boost your imagination.

Make certain to strap your seatbelts, my reader, for we are about to go on an incredible voyage. Guide " Mysteries Carved in Stones" is even more than simply a publication; it is an adventure into the depths of history, a look for understanding, and a party of the unyielding will of human questions. Join us as we check out the " Mysteries Carved in Stones" as well as discover the surprise truths, welcome the enigmas, and travel into the profound globe of the "Mysteries of Old Relics."

Introduction:

Mysteries Surrounding Ancient Relics

In the poorly lighted corridors of museums and also the dusty archaeological sites, the relics of our ancestors' past carefully draw us, whispering tales of long-lost worlds and knowledge that has been forgotten. There is a group of items within these sacred antiques that defy cognition and offer difficulty to our expertise in history, science, and the human spirit. These products are understood as "objects that oppose comprehension." Old artefacts as well as mysterious antiques from lost ages proceed to puzzle, plex, as well as enthral us. They are what we describe as the enigmatic old objects.

Imagine, if you will, a world in which history is not a collection of events in chronological order but rather an intricate tapestry that is weaved with hairs of interest and awe at every turn. Artefacts that work as mysterious guards and also secure enigmas that are beyond our understanding can be found woven into this tapestry. These artefacts, which have actually been dealt with by the hands of centuries-old craftsmen and also are instilled with the spirit of a bygone age, are home windows right into the midst of human ingenuity as well as the mysteries it hides.

Our adventure rejects the exploration of a mystical artefact recognized as the Antikythera System. This antique is so phenomenal that it compels us to review whatever we understand about the modern technology of past human beings. However, this is only the tip of the iceberg; it is a guard that guards the entry to a world loaded with unusual prizes, each of which has its very own mystery to be unravelled and its tricks to be disclosed.

We discover that we are drawn closer as well as better to the centre of the puzzle as we undergo the halls of time, where the shadows of the past dance and also resound with the mirrors of shed wisdom. The Antikythera Mechanism is an homage to human creation at the crossroads of science as well as the arts. It was discovered amid the Mediterranean Sea off the coast of the Greek island of Antikythera.

Envision that, at the bottom of the ocean, in the utter serenity of the abyss, there is a piece of bronze that has become coated with the antiques of time. The exploration of it in 1901 would trigger a chain response of inquiries, most of which have not been dealt with to today. It was an intricate collection of pieces of equipment and dials, and there was no chance to explain it. Was it a gizmo that aided with navigation? A calculator with huge features? A relic from a long-lost culture which contained information that was centuries ahead of its time?

As we set out on our journey, we will be navigating the dirty waters of opinion and also scepticism with the beam offered by our sense of marvel. We are most likely to check out the complexities of this old artefact with each other, as well as piece with each other the ideas that will certainly assist us in fixing its mystery. However, the Antikythera System is only the entrance indicating a globe full of other fascinating secrets. These mysteries are products that question our preconceived fertilizations of what was possible in times long ago.

The gorgeous geometry of the Great Pyramids of Giza opposes explanation, consequently, we will go across the deserts where they were developed hundreds of years back. We are going to see the strange Easter Island, which is home to the enormous Moai sculptures that stand to monitor the lore of the island's original citizens. The Lycurgus Cup is a chalice that moves colours as if it were had by the power of alchemy. We are most likely to analyze the subtle elegance of this mug in wonderful detail. As well as there, before us, will certainly exist the glistening Nazca Lines, carved right into the sands of the Peruvian desert and offering as a testimony to the people's goals towards the heavens.

However, our examination is not completed with these widely known mysteries. We are most likely to journey right into the domain name of the mystical as well as the confusing, such as the crystal skulls, which might or may not have come down from long-vanished worlds, the Piri Reis Map, which defies the recognised bounds of examination, and also the mysterious occurrences of the Baghdad Battery and the Stone Rounds of Costa Rica.

As we dive deeper into each of these mysteries, we will certainly not just be consulted with the sexy appeal of the unidentified, but likewise with the sticking around concerns that remain in the darkness. As we continue to explore each of these mysteries, we will come in person with both of these aspects. Were these artefacts the outcome of highly skilled human beings that have since disappeared? Were these presents from unusual entities that had been sent out to Earth in periods that were quiet in the past? Or were they the product of human creativity, the relics of a knowledge that flourished but is currently shed in the haze of time?

We will experience the fields of archaeology, background, physics, and also the occult in our look for answers, led by the understanding of scholars, the zeal of travellers, and also the insatiable inquisitiveness that binds all of us with each other. Each artefact that we come across will be an item of a jigsaw, a part of a better mosaic that both challenges our understanding of the past and encourages us to examine the possibilities that exist past it.

As we head out on this experience via time as well as the unidentified, we need to discover to be comfortable with uncertainty and also be impressed by the boldness of human query. Ancient artefacts are a homage to the eternal human spirit, which desires to address the secrets of the universes as well as the echoes of civilizations that have time out of mind disappeared, and also the enigma that borders these artefacts.

Join me, my readers, as we enter the labyrinth that is background, where the switching of each web page reveals a brand-new secret, a new barrier to our comprehension, and also a brand-new opportunity to check out the world of the unknown. Together, we will be able to open the doors of assumption as well as catch a peek at the marvels that are in store for those who are enduring sufficient to investigate the unanswered questions surrounding ancient artefacts.

CHAPTER 1: THE BAGHDAD BATTERY: PROOF OF ELECTRICITY IN ANCIENT TIMES?

A mysterious artefact was revealed in the dirty annals of Mesopotamia, which was as soon as the cradle of civilisation. This relic questions our understanding of the background and also tips on the capacity of advanced technology growing in the ancient past. Mesopotamia was once the residence of the city of Ur, which is thought to be the birthplace of people. This is the story of the Baghdad Battery, a simple clay jar that has triggered debate concerning exactly how well old people recognized electrical energy.

Imagine the completely dry plains of contemporary Iraq, which were previously home to prospering historical towns. These levels are where Iraq is currently. The Tigris and the Euphrates rivers both streamed via this area, giving a fertile setting for the development of worlds that were accountable for the creation of the wheel, composing, and farming. Excavators were performing excavations in the remains of these once-great cities when they made a search that would spark a discussion that would last for centuries.

The year was 1936, and the German excavator Wilhelm Konig was digging into the damages of the Parthian town of Khujut Rabu, which lay near Baghdad. While he and his colleagues were fastidiously excavating the remains of a lost age, they encountered an appealing discovery: a little clay container that gave the impact of being average in the outdoors, yet within was something that would certainly ignite the interest of academics with amateurs.

It was difficult to discuss the collection of artefacts that were located within the container. Copper and iron rods, a copper cylinder, and an asphalt stopper comprised the vessel's closure device. These points might have appeared irrelevant to the inexperienced eye, like the leftovers from an old workshop or the outcomes of an experiment that was long earlier forgotten. In the hands of those who knew their meaning, they were a key that opened a door to a strange and wonderful world.

When checked out more attentively, the copper cylindrical tube showed a finish of rust, which gave the appearance of an aged patina and spoke to the flow of time. It wasn't the artefact's classical times that ignited the interest of the academics; rather, it was the appealing prospect of what the things were utilized for. Is it feasible that this clay jar, with each other with its contents, previously worked as an old battery?

The idea of an old battery provides a difficulty to the accepted account of historic events as well as tips that our precursors may have had a much deeper grasp of power than was formerly intended. The inquiry, which looms like a tornado coming up, is as follows: Could the Baghdad Battery have been made use of in the ancient globe as a vessel for taking advantage of electric power?

Before we can continue any kind of further right into the midst of this mystery, we need to obtain a much better grasp of the scientific research that underpins the concept. Electrons moving via a conductor trigger the phenomenon that we describe as power. It is the driving force behind whatever composes our modern environment, from the lights that illuminate our homes to the digital gadgets that connect us to the internet world. However, the idea of electrical power did not constantly exist within the realm of human understanding. It was necessary to initially uncover it, then comprehend it, and after that place it to utilize.

It forces us to review the order in which electrical inventions took place if this is the purpose of the Baghdad Battery. Individuals like Benjamin Franklin as well as Alessandro Volta, who carried out pioneering experiments in the 18th and 19th centuries, are typically considered as individuals who are in charge of the development of modern-day power. What if the old Mesopotamians had found anything equivalent to our present understanding thousands of years earlier?

To investigate this option, we will be required to take a look at the parts that comprise the Baghdad Battery. When a service that was either acidic or alkaline was included in the copper cylindrical tube, it could act as an electrolyte, which is a medium where ions might stream. After being placed within the cylinder, the iron rod would certainly have acted as an anode, while the copper rod would have played the duty of a cathode. When it is linked to an outdoor conductor, the configuration can produce an electric current.

The repercussions of this discovery are fairly substantial. If it ends up that the Baghdad Battery was an old electric tool, then it is intriguing to hypothesize regarding the features it might have executed in the past. It has been hypothesised that it may have been utilized for electroplating, which is the procedure of covering products with extremely slim layers of metal. Some people believe that it may have had a spiritual or clinical purpose and that it may have also had the ability to administer electric shocks for either medicinal or ceremonial reasons.

A fascinating concept suggests that the Baghdad Battery was formerly utilized to brighten old cities. This relatively little artefact might have been used to power lamps or other kinds of sources of light, giving a look of modern innovation in the centre of ancient times. If it were verified that old worlds had electric lights, it would certainly throw our present view of the background and also the advancement of human creative thinking into inquiry.

As we move further down the route of examination, we will likewise need to encounter the sceptics as well as the unresolved problems that add to the mystique around the Baghdad Battery. There is inadequate evidence, according to its critics, to effectively show that the things concerned feature as an electrical tool. They keep in mind that there are no cable televisions or connectors present, which prevents the tool from being integrated right into a broader electric network.

On top of that, several researchers have recommended alternating interpretations for the artefacts that were uncovered in Khujut Rabu. They theorise that the cylindrical item made from copper may have been a receptacle for the storage space of divine scrolls or a vessel for the storage space of papyrus or paper. They believe that the iron as well as copper poles might have been used to support these scrolls, which would have allowed them to be rolled up and kept even more quickly.

As we make our method via the uneven seas of this conversation, we have little option but to accept the secret that borders the Baghdad Battery. It is a conundrum that both teases as well as baffles us, a challenge that urges us to test the limitations of both our knowledge and our imagination. It's feasible that the reality of its function will certainly never be fully revealed to us, which would certainly be a suitable tribute to the ever-present secret of history.

As we continue to seek comprehension, we are reminded words of Socrates, the ancient Greek theorist, who stated that "wisdom starts in marvel." The Baghdad Battery urges us to speculate concerning the breadth and depth of human knowledge in times long gone, in addition to the extraordinary creativity that might have continued the darkness of history.

My lovely readers, as we continue our expedition further into the mystical artefact we are exploring looking for responses that may never be revealed to us. It is a voyage that pushes the restrictions of what is feasible and encourages us to consider the tricks that continue to exist hidden underneath the sands of time.

CHAPTER 2: THE ANTIKYTHERA MECHANISM - AN ANCIENT COMPUTER?

In the summertime of 1901, a group of Greek sponge scuba divers triggered on a hazardous voyage right into the midsts of the Mediterranean Sea. Their location was unidentified. They looked for good luck in the shape of sea sponges listed below the azure waters, at the boundary between Poseidon's domain name as well as the world of the living. They had no concept that their expedition of the ocean below would bring about the discovery of a relic that would certainly reverberate through the record of history and also transform the narrative of human accomplishment. This antique was a prize that was much more considerable than any type of sponge could offer.

The divers were unprepared for the wonder that greeted them as they went down into the dirty depths of the void that let go of the rough shore of the island of Antikythera, which is situated in Greece. In the middle of the murky domain of sunken ships and aquatic life, their eyes fell upon things that frustrated their understanding. It was a rusted mass of metal and equipment that had been knotted in the arms of time. Antikythera Device was the globe's very first understood analogue computer system, and this plain artefact, which had been recovered from the midsts of oblivion, would soon become called the Antikythera System.

Envision, if you will, a world that existed even more than 2,000 years earlier which was characterised by the sun-dappled shores of the Mediterranean being including life as well as society. Ancient Greek thinkers and researchers were stars in the areas of ideology as well as science. They wondered at the sky and also looked to decipher the secrets of the universe. Plato and Aristotle, 2 of the most influential philosophers of perpetuity, were energetic in the city-states of Athens and Alexandria. Eratosthenes established the circumference of the Earth.

In the centre of all of this intellectual commotion, there was a puzzle-- an incredible mystery that called into inquiry the standard properties upon which they based their comprehension. The movements of the sky, the cycles of the stars, as well as the intricacy of the lunar calendar all continued to be an enigma that challenged the most brilliant minds of old times.

The Antikythera Device is a residue that demonstrates the guts of human query and also the inventiveness of our precursors. It was found on the island of Antikythera in Greece. Within this intricate framework rests the core of a machine, a machine that seems to hold the possibility to comprehend the mysteries of the cosmos itself. In the beginning appearance, it might look like a pile of tarnished metal, a mess of little bits and pieces of equipment.

Allow us, as we depend on the brink of fixing this olden enigma, to set out on a trip of exploration, one that will check our expertise in history and science along with the limits of what is possible for people to do. Inside the Antikythera Mechanism, we discover the materialisation of an olden wish-- a dream to understand deep space and also to use its understanding for the innovation of humanity.

The whole suggestion of an antique computer system is antiquated, like a rumour tweezed from the pages of a sci-fi story. It is tough to comprehend in this day as well as age, when we all lug the capacity of computation in our pockets, that such a level of knowledge might have been there in the remote past. Despite this, as we go deeper into the past, we are most likely to find some tantalising evidence that points to the presence of a technology that was centuries in advance of its time.

The Antikythera System is a jigsaw challenge that is composed of dials, engravings, and gears. It was discovered in the wreckage of a ship that diminished the coastline of Antikythera in the year 60 BCE. The ship, which was a vessel from the Hellenistic period, lugged the cargo of a past age, which included opulent sculptures, pottery, and also amphorae filled to the complete with the wealth of a disappeared world. However it was the system, a little as well as an unremarkable-looking section of the haul, that would become the most appealing element of the locate.

Envision the minute when this piece of the background was tweezed from the depths of the sea, still encrusted with the barnacles that time as well as salinity had based on it. What arose from the depths of the pit was not a spectacular prize chest overflowing with cash and valuable rocks. Instead, it was a simple collection of bronze cogs, some of which were no larger than a thumb, interlaced in a style that suggested a function that was much past the reach of the average individual's creative imagination.

It was throughout the process of delivering the artefact to the National Archaeological Museum of Athens that it first began disclosing its secrets. Archaeologists and scientists, fascinated by the problem before them, established out on a trip to address the system's riddles and reveal its tricks. They were captivated by the precise creativity that had gone into its growth; it was workmanship that mentioned a civilisation with a degree of comprehension that had been unimaginable as much as that factor.

The Antikythera System is made up of an intricate collection of gears, several of which have as many as 223 teeth. These gears are thoroughly meshed together in a fashion that can be considered absolutely nothing much less than a piece of mechanical wizard. Its writings, which were carved on the surface of the bronze casing it was housed in, provided interesting insights. Words such as "Meton" and "Callippus" supplied hints to the identities of old astronomers and mathematicians, while intimations to the cycles of the moon and the planets offered hints at the features that it performed in the universes.

Our trip into the core of the mechanism does not formally begin until we have reached this stage. The problems that are brought up are quite crucial and also facility. What feature did these antiquated devices play in the past? Just how were its designers able to obtain the understanding and experience necessary to create such a complex machine? What discoveries regarding the world did it have to offer? Why did the expertise of this technology vanish from the annals of the background, leaving just this mysterious artefact as a monolith of its existence? This is arguably one of the most difficult concerns of all.

The whole concept of anything being an "old computer" is perplexing per se. In a world where computer systems conjure visions of silicon chips and also electronic codes, the principle of an analogue instrument that might reproduce the motions of holy bodies may feel like a far-fetched fantasy. The Antikythera Mechanism, on the other hand, does not fit well into any preexisting classifications, as we will certainly see in a minute. It is a beaming example of the ingenuity of those who offered it birth and also acted as a guidepost to info in a period that is currently long gone.

As a component of our efforts to analyze the secrets of the Antikythera System, we will need to translucent the haze of time, take a look at the antiques of a vanished human being, as well as make our way into the centre of a riddle. It is a voyage that will certainly check our understanding of background, science, as well as the creativity of humans, and it will certainly get us to the point where we will certainly have to encounter the suggestion that the ancients possessed knowledge and technology that was much more innovative than we have ever agreed to contemplate.

Dear viewers, as we continue further right into the bowels of this age-old enigma, The rusted remains of the Antikythera System contain a story that extends beyond the boundaries of time; it is a tale of inquisitiveness, resourcefulness, and also the never-ending pursuit to figure out the enigmas of deep space.

CHAPTER 3: ASTRONOMY AND CALENDAR FUNCTIONS: CLUES FROM THE GEARS

We progress farther right into the core of the Antikythera Mechanism while ensconced in the silent acceptance of time's secrets. The secret becomes more bewildering as time goes on, simply as how the incredible tapestry proceeds to unfold above us. It is here, in the complicated gears as well as dials, that the mutterings of ancient astronomers and calendar-keepers find voice; a voice that calls us to decipher the incredible mysteries that are housed within this old marvel.

As we proceed further right into the puzzle of the Antikythera Device, the profound details it includes are the first point we need to get to grips with before proceeding with our exploration. Think of that you are in the chamber of an ancient observatory, which is dimly lit, as well as the dome of the observatory is painted with the stars that have offered as a map for humankind over the ages. This celestial tapestry, which is a cosmic symphony of celebrities and worlds, as well as time and area, is what the Antikythera System is trying to capture.

The beyond the system is stealthily small; it includes a bronze instance that has been stained by the caring treatment of centuries, and behind that, a system of gears is hidden. However, when we examine its difficult internal workings, we can see that it is a depiction of the cosmos made out of metal and rock. The equipment is of diverse sizes, as well as they fit with each other with such accuracy that their teeth are taken part in a divine dancing that was choreographed centuries ago. It is a harmony of mechanical ingenuity, where the activity of each gear is tuned to the heavens themselves.

Our trip starts with the principle of time considering that in the old globe, time was not measured in simple seconds and minutes but instead by the rhythms of the universes as well as the celestial bodies in the cosmos. The Antikythera Device is a cosmic clockwork that monitors the movements of the skies with astonishing accuracy; it is a homage to the timeless knowledge that has been passed down through the ages.

This old wonder was not a straightforward clock but rather a celestial calculator, a device that could expect huge occurrences with remarkable accuracy. As we analyze its type of equipment, we are concerned to comprehend that this old marvel was not a straightforward wristwatch but rather a celestial calculator. It was a device that provided its customers with the capacity to see into the future, see the dance of worlds and celebrities, predict eclipses as well as solstices, and also observe the passing of time with wonder and reverence.

The type of equipment that we see rotating within the Antikythera Device resembles the gears that work throughout the cosmos itself; they kip down perfect consistency to collaborate the movements of divine bodies. The larger gears are meant to illustrate the cyclical nature of time, specifically the day-to-day, monthly, and yearly landmarks that form our lives. They are the cosmic metronomes that determine the pulse of the universe.

However, it is the smaller pieces of equipment that are naturally nested inside the system's core that demonstrate the real breadth as well as deepness of its planetary expertise. Each piece of equipment bears an intricate inscription that portrays a zodiac sign in addition to a heavenly body, such as the sunlight, the moon, or the planets. These inscriptions are done with the utmost precision. They are the methods whereby the enigmas of the universe might be uncovered, given that the options to the puzzles of ancient astronomy can be discovered embedded within the cycles of their turnings.

Picture, if you will, the old astronomer who spun the dials of the Antikythera Device to line the types of equipment with the placements of the planets. This was performed to produce the Antikythera Mechanism. Throughout each revolution, he adjusted the mechanism's calibration to a brand-new day, bringing it into step with the cosmic ballet that was taking location above. And also as he cranked the handle, the equipment clicked and also whirred, drawing up the orbits of the planets throughout the cosmos.

The Antikythera Device provided its customers the capacity to forecast not just the stages of the moon but also the areas of the earth, such as Mercury, Venus, Mars, Jupiter, as well as Saturn. It was a celestial almanack, a gold mine of expensive information that lighted the night sky for those who held its keys. Those who possessed its keys were able to see everything in the evening skies.

The actual secret of this old artefact relaxes not just in its skill to calculate expensive events, but additionally in its ability to reconcile the solar and lunar schedules. This is what makes it so impressive. The difference between these 2 calendars was a difficulty on the planet of classical times, and it was one that priests, as well as pundits alike, found challenging to overcome. The Antikythera System, on the other hand, provided an option in the form of a synchronised merging of time that brought the lunar months as well as the solar year into appropriate placement.

When thinking about the relevance of this achievement, it is essential to keep in mind that the Antikythera System was created centuries before the current calendar. It is a credit rating to the ancient people's knowledge that they made every effort to bridge the space between the solar as well as lunar cycles to ensure the equilibrium of time itself.

We can virtually construct the mutterings of old astronomers as we rest here in the serenity of our reflection and also consider them. Their voices have been carried along by the currents of time. They were the keepers of holy knowledge and also the guardians of the cosmos, and they left us with the Antikythera Mechanism, a planetary enigma that remains to check our understanding of the past and the limitless depths of human inquiry.

As we come to the end of this phase and prepare to check out additionally right into the tricks of this phenomenal artefact, let us ponder the words of Carl Sagan: "We are star-stuff contemplating the stars." The Antikythera Mechanism is a representation of humankind's inherent impulse to understand deep space, to map the skies, as well as to address the riddles of time itself. It offers a tip that the ambitions of the human soul have continued via the ages, also right into the depths of antiquity.

CHAPTER 4:
THE VOYNICH MANUSCRIPT: A CHALLENGING ENCRYPTION PROBLEM

A residue of indecipherable enigma may be located in the poorly lighted archives of the Beinecke Rare Publication & Document Collection at Yale University. This relic is a file that has stumped one of the most brilliant minds and escaped the most figured-out codebreakers for hundreds of years. It is referred to as the Voynich Manuscript, and it is a perplexing puzzle that invites us right into the labyrinth of an old language, a failed-to-remember body of understanding and a quandary that will not reveal its solutions.

When we initially get in the globe of the Voynich Manuscript, we are promptly struck by exactly how otherworldly it shows up to be. Envision a book that resists classification, its web pages loaded with a language that has never been deciphered, surrounded with illustrations of plants that defy botanical classification and figures that negate human anatomy. This book would be difficult to classify. It is a remnant that floats at the limit between what is known as well as what is unknown, and also it is an homage to the long-lasting pressure of human interest.

The actual text is a humble book, with its web pages made from vellum as well as bound in such a way that is straightforward yet appealing. Hidden past its moderate exterior is a globe of remarkable and mystical things. Guide, which was written in an unidentified script and has been provided with the name Voynichese, is a homage to the secrets that are fundamental in the language itself. The personalities move over the web page with a grace that betrays their incomprehensible nature, like a ballet of heavy icons that torture our capacity for comprehension.

The opening couple of pages of the book are covered with illustrations of plants, yet none of these plants can be correctly identified according to their agricultural characteristics. They have an otherworldly appearance, nearly as if a wild botanist had been dreaming about them. There are ways in which the fallen leaves and the roots are intertwined that violate the basic policies of nature. Were these plants fictitious or the outcome of an overactive imagination for the musician? For ages, this question has given stress to academics.

Nevertheless, the complicated flora in the Voynich Manuscript does not complete the riddles in this old paper. As we turn the web pages, we are consulted with a gallery of characters, including nude women saturating in strange waters as well as animals from other worlds romping among the cryptic language. The human numbers, with their elongated bodies and expressions that share a feeling of mystery, seem beings from various other dimensions or aeroplanes of existence.

The Voynich Manuscript is a problem with chroniclers, cryptographers, and linguists similarly baffled. It is a harmony of the strange, a tapestry of the inexplicable, and also a job that has stunned them all. Its beginnings and reasons for existing are hidden in obscurity at this moment. Who is the author? When was it initially provided? What details does it hold, and also why was it written in such a mysterious style in the first location?

Among the initially recognized references to the Voynich Manuscript returns to the 17th century, when it entered into the possession of the Czech sorcerer and bibliophile Georg Baresch. This is among the earliest known recommendations for the Voynich Manuscript. Even throughout his lifetime, the job had an online reputation for being puzzling. In the contact that he had with others, Baresch described it as "a puzzle that no person on the planet will be able to solve."

After passing via the hands of Baresch, the manuscript made its way right into the ownership of the Jesuit scholar Athanasius Kircher. Kircher was a man who was widely known for his profound passion regarding the all-natural world as well as the mystical. Kircher, in his quest for understanding, made an effort to understand the handwriting and also find the concealed meanings in the book. He found himself perplexed by the incomprehensible content of the record, simply like lots of that came previously and after him.

The old book merchant Wilfrid Voynich, who wanted puzzling and odd writings, was the one that eventually came into the belongings of the manuscript around the turn of the 20th century. He would certainly go on to end up being the person whose name would be provided in the book. Voynich, who was enthralled by the secrets consisted of in the paper, dedicated his whole life to examining and securing them.

Nevertheless, despite Voynich's finest efforts as well as the subsequent initiatives of a substantial variety of experts, the writing is still unintelligible, and the situations surrounding its beginnings proceed to be shrouded in secret. The Voynich Manuscript has been associated with everybody from mediaeval sorcerers to Renaissance polymaths, and its aim has been believed to vary from a sophisticated trick to a book on organic medication. There is a plethora of concepts surrounding the Voynich Manuscript, yet none are definitive.

One of the most tempting attributes of the Voynich Manuscript is the concept that it includes info that has been concealed; information that, if analyzed, can completely change our perspective on the past. Some people believe that it might open long-forgotten languages, long-forgotten cyphers, or hitherto taboo clinical fields. The manuscript has been analysed using advanced technologies such as ultraviolet imaging and spectroscopy to uncover previously unidentified layers of text or significance.

Despite all of these efforts, the Voynich Manuscript proceeds to act as a watchful watchdog over its contents. It is a demo of the perseverance of human curiosity as well as the ever-present allure of the obscure. The pursuit of expertise is not always concerning locating remedies; rather, it is about inviting the questions that take us into undiscovered areas. As we depend on the brink of this puzzle, we are reminded that the quest for expertise is not always concerned with finding responses.

When we explore the Voynich Manuscript, we must keep in mind the words of Socrates, the fantastic Greek thinker, who once proclaimed, "All I know is that I recognize nothing." The message forces us to analyze the legitimacy of our presumptions, to recognize the boundaries of our understanding, and to consider the immensity of the enigmas that border us.

As we proceed to turn the pages of this phase and also prepare to dig even better right into the secret bordering the Voynich Manuscript, allow us not to neglect that the search for understanding is not an individual effort but rather a cumulative one that covers both time and also space. The text is a difficulty to the analytical minds of the past, present, as well as future; it is a puzzle that encourages us to join the ranks of those who have ventured to travel right into the mysterious unknown.

Join me, as we try to decode the enigmas that are hidden inside the Voynich Manuscript by navigating its complex script and also attempting to identify what all of it ways. It is a voyage filled with hazards, but it is also one that urges us to succumb to the tempting attraction of the strange as well as the undiscovered.

CHAPTER 5: THE SEARCH FOR CRYPTOGRAPHERS

In the murky annals of history, a limited handful of people have risen to the remarkable task of the Voynich Manuscript. This is a difficulty that has actually astonished generations and also sustained the flames of interest in several of the greatest minds of our time. They are the cryptographers, the codebreakers, and the etymological sages that have ventured to battle with the cryptic writing of the Voynichese manuscript to uncover its mysteries.

Throughout attempting to decode the Voynich message, a cast of individualities with backgrounds nearly as varied as the text itself has arisen. This cryptographic task has been tackled by a variety of individuals, including academics, linguists, computer researchers, and amateur cryptanalysts alike. Each individual has used their unique set of abilities and perspectives to the centuries-old challenge, and they have done so with dogged willpower to address the puzzle and uncover its concealed details.

The story of cryptographers and their search began with William Romaine Newbold, a brilliant but controversial professor of ideology at the University of Pennsylvania in the early 20th century. The Voynich Manuscript was one of the earliest messages that Newbold attempted to translate, as well as he was among the very first individuals to do so seriously. His technique was original along with being rather strong.

Newbold assumed that the Voynichese message was not composed in any well-known language but was rather inscribed making use of a complicated system of acronyms, anagrams, and also sign control. He believed this since the Voynichese language is not connected to any type of various other recognized language. His examination, which was based upon complex astrological and alchemical interpretations, led him to the conclusion that the record consisted of substantial insights worrying both the nature of the world as well as the significance of existence itself.

Even though Newbold's theories brought in a great deal of individuals's interest and also got a great deal of individuals assuming artistically, in the end, they were received with scepticism as well as criticism. Some others felt that his approach was based upon much conjecture as well as relied too greatly on the writer's own choices. Due to the odd nature of the record, it was open to a broad selection of analyses, and Newbold's ideas were not able to offer a definitive solution to the issue.

William Friedman, a widely known cryptanalyst who was crucial in the decipherment of the Purple cypher utilized by the Japanese during World Battle II, will be liable for the following phase of the cryptographic search. At the tail end of the 1940s, Friedman started concentrating his interest on the Voynich Manuscript. He started by systematically examining the message inside the record, armed with the massive knowledge he had obtained in the art of understanding secret messages.

The Voynichese message was attacked by Friedman and his better half Elizebeth, who was also a notable codebreaker in her very own right. They did this by utilizing rigorous statistical analysis. They were seeking recurring motifs as well as circumstances, in addition to analytical outliers, in the hopes that they could use tips concerning the underlying structure of the movie script. Even with their meticulous efforts, the record proceeded to be incomprehensible.

As even more time passed, a boosting variety of linguists and cryptographers were associated with the search. These individuals brought with them their distinctive techniques and concepts. Others considered linguistic parallels with various other well-known languages, while others focused on analytical research study of the language. Some individuals believed that the writing was a made-up language or a very encrypted version of a known language, while others believed that it was a code hiding essential info.

The text was believed to have a mnemonic system, which is a device for an author to remember details without needing to compose them directly. This was just one of the theories put up. Others conjectured that it was just an imaginative production, an item of abstract art that had no feature apart from standing for the artist's visual sensibilities.

The Voynich Manuscript's surprise meanings have escaped decipherment despite the numerous methods that have been tried and the steadfast dedication of the cryptographers who have serviced it. The composing resisted etymological classification, the analytical research study produced unclear findings, and the evasive cypher that veiled its significance proceeded to stay clear of decoding.

The search for a decryption trick to the Voynich Manuscript continues to be continuous even in the contemporary, with fresh generations of codebreakers climbing to satisfy the challenge. The advent of modern technology has given the endeavour sophisticated tools and boosted handling capability, which has made it feasible to carry out nuanced as well as comprehensive research studies of the text as well as illustrations consisting of inside guides.

The Voynichese message was recently evaluated with the usage of fabricated knowledge as well as machine-knowing algorithms, which caused one substantial advancement. The researchers created semantic networks to acknowledge patterns and correlations within the screenplay with the aim that a computer would reveal insights that go beyond human understanding. Although these attempts have produced some interesting explorations, they have not yet led to a final decryption.

The Voynich Manuscript has been as well as will certainly remain to be considered the peak of a problem for cryptographers; it is a tantalising mystery that opposes any type and all efforts to solve it. It is a monument to the endless depths of human inquisitiveness and also the unceasing search for understanding. The mirrors of a long-forgotten knowledge may be discovered within its pages, patiently waiting for the day when the cypher will at long last be figured out as well as its secrets will be made public.

When we finally leave the cryptographers and also their perpetual search behind, we are entrusted to the unsettling words of the great codebreaker Alan Turing: "Occasionally it is the individuals nobody can envision anything of that do the things no one can think of." The effort to decipher the Voynich Manuscript is a monolith of the persevering spirit of people who dare to dream the unthinkable and to check out the unknown frontiers of human expertise.

As we go further right into the centre of this confusing puzzle, where the echoes of the previous mingle with the hopes of the future, and also where the ceaseless search of expertise proceeds to brighten the way to discovery.

CHAPTER 6: NANOTECHNOLOGY IN ANTIQUITY? A LOOK AT THE LYCURGUS CUP.

An antique Roman chalice is an artefact that has captured the imaginations of scientists, researchers, and art fanatics alike. It may be found hidden in the depths of the British Museum, where it is surrounded by a treasure trove of old artefacts. This outstanding mug, which has been provided the name the Lycurgus Mug, invites us to enter into the past and also ponder the adhering to concern: Could the secrets of nanotechnology have been taken advantage of in antiquity?

To get started on our journey, we are required to initially return in time to the days of the Roman Realm. During that era, artisans, artisans, as well as designers were pushing the limitations of what was feasible in terms of innovation. The courts of nobles, as well as emperors, were outdoors decked with beneficial metals and rare rocks throughout this time around duration, which was a time of great uniqueness as well as prosperity. Nonetheless, in the centre of every one of this majesty, the Lycurgus Mug continues to be a statement to a kind of imagination that is extra downplayed and mysterious.

Envision, if you will, a container constructed from clear eco-friendly glass, imbued with an aerial lustre that opposes the policies of nature. This thing would certainly be impossible to discover in nature. The surface of the cup is covered with beautiful alleviation styles that reflect the mythological tale of King Lycurgus. When viewed in natural light, the mug sparkles with an evocative jade brightness. The domain of darkness is where the real power of the Lycurgus Mug can manifest itself and also function its wonders.

The chalice undergoes a spectacular change as night drops as well as the ambient light in the chamber comes to be dimmer. The once-green glass transforms into a fantastic colour of scarlet, giving off a glow that seems to originate from somewhere weird. It is practically as if the mug had a life of its own, with a strange light resource hidden somewhere deep within its inside. The outcome is nothing brief of mesmerising, as well as it is a sensation that has fascinated and perplexed academics for decades.

The extraordinary craftsmanship that entered into making the Lycurgus Mug is the key to opening the mystery behind its mesmerising adjustment. As we take a look at the surface area of the mug in further deepness, we find that its colouring is not the result of an uncomplicated mix of dyes as well as pigments. Instead, it is an accomplishment of ancient nanotechnology, a great display screen of submicron-scale metal bits implanted inside the glass matrix. This is an instance of old nanotechnology at its finest.

The ancient Roman glassmakers were able to complete this

incredible achievement by following a very specific treatment. They began with a structure of clear glass that was infused with extremely fine particles of silver and gold. Because these bits were minimized down to a dimension smaller than a wavelength of visible light, when they were similarly distributed within the glass they were not visible to the human eye. The chameleon-like qualities of the Lycurgus Cup can be credited to the mindful control that was exercised on the size of the nanoparticles as well as their distribution.

When light travels with the glass, it comes into contact with these extremely minute metal bits, which can uniquely take in as well as reemit particular wavelengths of light. The glass handles a green tone when lit up by natural light as an outcome of a process referred to as localised surface plasmon vibration. When lit from behind or by a light resource included within the cup itself, the nanoparticles connect with the incoming light to give a crimson colour. This is an amazing program of optical magic that should have left old revellers in wonder.

The Lycurgus Mug is more than simply a masterpiece; it is evidence of the originality of artists who had a comprehensive understanding of the materials they dealt with and the qualities of those products. It calls into inquiry our presumptions about the degree of complexity of old innovation and motivates us to reconsider the limits of nanotechnology's usage in the ancient world.

While we can't yet be mesmerized by the fantastic beauty of the Lycurgus Mug and the nanoscale wonders concealed behind its glass, we likewise need to ask ourselves what the factor of this impressive production is. Why did the Romans put a lot of effort and time into creating a chalice that had optical qualities that were so perplexing?

There is a college of thought that recommends the Lycurgus Mug was created to be an item of distinction and luxury; even more especially, an amazing centrepiece for royal feasts and festivities. In line with the fabulous story revealed in the relief designs on its surface area, its changing homes, which included a change from green to red, might have been meant to stand for principles connected to rebirth, metamorphosis, and the passage of time.

Some people believe that the mug served a ritualistic or ritualistic duty during religious observations, with its changing colours producing a feeling of divine participation or otherworldly happenings. This concept is shared by others. The ancient Romans, like lots of other old people, had an extensive respect for the magical as well as the superordinary. Due to its incredible qualities, the Lycurgus Cup may have been used in spiritual settings to evoke feelings of awe as well as awe in the faithful.

Scholars continue to say and hypothesize concerning the actual function of the Lycurgus Mug; yet, this does not change the fact that it remains to be a subject of interest. It is a tribute to the varied character of ancient artefacts, which often evade easy categorization and resist being explained simply.

As we proceed to check out the Lycurgus Mug, we find ourselves significantly curious about the methods by which technology, scientific research, and art intersected in the old world. We are reminded that the wonders of nanotechnology were not the sole building of the modern period; rather, it is feasible that our ancestors checked out as well as understood them in a manner ins which proceeded to impress as well as influence us today.

As we come to the end of this phase and obtain all set to dive better into the enigmas of the past, let us consider the words of the fantastic Roman poet Ovid, who wrote, "I am birthed,/

Birthed as I stare: below my feet the planet/ Autumns back, and skies unvisited by cloud/ Introduce their starry secrets." As we come to the end of this chapter and also prepare ourselves to dig much deeper into the enigmas of the past, let us assess these words. The Lycurgus Mug extends an invite to us to stare into the starry mysteries of the vintage, where even one of the most fundamental chalices can conceal wonders that are past our wildest imaginings.

CHAPTER 7: CAN THE STONE SPHERES OF COSTA RICA BE LINKED TO GIANTS WHO CARVED THEM?

In the centre of the green rain forests of Costa Rica, under the emerald canopy where jaguars prowl and scarlet macaws dance, there is a profound enigma inscribed in rock. It includes massive spheres that are flawlessly shaped and also strangely attractive, and they are spread throughout the terrain like marbles. These strange artefacts are referred to as the Rock Rounds of Costa Rica, and also they invite us to ponder the actual nature of their existence along with the tales that are said to be associated with them.

As we go deeper right into the rainforests of Costa Rica, we rate a scene that is rupturing with life. It looks as though the towering trees and rich vegetation are weaving a living tapestry around the rock balls and cradling them in their arms. This verdant embrace is where we obtain our first experience with these old secrets; the sheer size and symmetry of these structures resist the mind.

Think of for a minute that you are checking out a stone round that coincides with elevation as a person and also considers the same amount as an elephant. These rounds have been shaped from the very bedrock of the ground, as well as they demonstrate a sensational perfection that is so specific that it almost looks magical. Their surfaces are brightened to the point that they appear like mirrors, their types are ideal balls, and the fact that they are aligned with celestial incidents like the equinoxes shows that they have a wonderful understanding of astronomy.

Nevertheless, the excellence of their handiwork is not the only thing that baffles us about them. In the muggy air of the forest, there is a relentless mystery about their feature as well as where they came from. How did these enormous spheres come to be, and why was such painstaking focus on detail placed right into their production?

The indigenous people of Costa Rica, who resided in these regions for a lengthy period before Europeans showed up, are the subjects of one suggestion that suggests they were the ones who initially produced the stone balls. This notion, however, has been lost in the mists of time. This theory suggests that the rounds were utilized as monoliths or marks to signify authority, ceremonial relevance, or geographical boundaries. In factor of truth, the ancient cultures of the region had extensive understanding of astronomy as well as geometry. It is feasible that the spheres were aligned with divine areas or divine incidents.

When we examine the aboriginal roots of the rock balls, nonetheless, the size of the job handy comes to be promptly evident to us. Exactly how were these old civilizations able to move and make stone balls of such massive dimensions as well as weight without the assistance of modern technology? Our knowledge of the capacities of these ancient cultures is challenged by the incredible amount of planning and preparation that would certainly be needed for such an endeavour.

One additional idea, one that has stimulated the rate of interest of several individuals, proposes that the rock balls have a more otherworldly origin. This concept is a principle that evokes the presence of ancient giants or extraterrestrial beings as the individuals who were in charge of their development. The large dimension of the spheres as well as their determined accuracy are cited as proof of a level of modern technology and virtuosity that was past the abilities of early human people by advocates of this suggestion.

The opportunity that the rounds were fashioned by big beings or were a gift to humankind from technically skilled alien visitors inspires feelings of awe as well as awe. It summons ideas of massive beings toiling away in the depths of the jungle, shaping stone with an ability past that of human beings, and sharing the understanding they acquired from their journeys to various other globes with the inhabitants of Earth.

As we go further right into the enigmas bordering the rock balls, we are required to think about the difficulties that modern excavators and scholars challenge when trying to decipher the spheres' concealed meanings. Both the treacherous topography of the thick forest and the relentless passage of time have functioned with each other to cover the real range of these old secrets. A lot of the spheres are still entombed under the surface of the planet, where they remain safeguarded from prying eyes and also patiently wait to disclose their enigmas to those who are brave sufficient to discover them.

Historical digs as well as study tasks have helped drop some understanding of the origins of the rock balls and the role they served. It is believed that the outstanding craftsmanship of the native cultures of Costa Rica, particularly the Diqus, was accomplished by making use of an approach known as "rock quarrying" or "pecking." This required the usage of labour-intensive rock devices, sand, as well as water to carve and grind items of igneous rock.

It's possible that the balls were created throughout several generations, with each community making a payment for the procedure. After being sculpted, the rounds were transferred to the websites where they were meant to pass employing a range of approaches, including rolling, leveraging, as well as water transport, using the area's comprehensive network of rivers and tributaries.

In close distance to a variety of the stone round locations, current investigations have revealed the existence of petroglyphs in addition to various other archaeological features. According to the searchings, the balls may have been used as markers or focal points for ritualistic as well as common conferences. These occasions would have remained by the old people's spiritual as well as astrological ideas.

Despite these explorations, the rock spheres continue to resist straightforward classification. They remain to be representations of both the inventiveness of people and also the appeal of the mysterious unknown. We are invited to explore the worlds of myth and reality, of ancient knowledge and also mystical starts, as the mystery surrounding their genesis and also purpose continues to be disclosed piece by piece.

We are advised of the words of the renowned American writer Henry David Thoreau as we work towards getting an understanding of the Stone Rounds of Costa Rica. Henry David Thoreau as soon as said, "It is not what you consider that issue; it is what you see." The stone spheres, which are pointed as peaceful sentinels in the centre of the rainforest, press us not only to see but also to see; they ask us to gaze behind the surface area of the rock as well as right into the midsts of humans background, where tales, as well as unresolved puzzles, combine.

Allow us, as we come to the end of this chapter and prepare to dig additionally right into the mysteries that exist at the core of these old challenges, to embrace the feeling of marvel as well as interest that they stimulate in us. The Stone Spheres of Costa Rica are a reminder that the past is a gold mine of mysteries that are waiting to be found by those who have the nerve to seek them out. They are a tribute to the proceeding spirit of exploration and exploration that has been given through the ages.

CHAPTER 8: THE STONE SPHERES OF COSTA RICA: UNLOCKING THE MYSTERIES CONCEALED

Our interest in the Stone Spheres just continues to grow as we venture even more into the heart of the jungle in Costa Rica. These enormous rounds, each of which is a tribute to the lingering enigmas of antiquity, have a way of getting the creativity while concurrently resolutely declining to reveal their surprise definitions. As we continue our investigation, we will certainly dive more right into the intricacy of these mystical stones and the persistent stories that border them. This will be the second part of our investigation.

The large selection of the Stone Spheres is among the most distinctive attributes of these strange objects. Also though the bulk of these stone wonders take the kind of balls, their sizes vary from just a few inches to as much as nearly eight feet. The colour, texture, and makeup of each ball are various from the others, and there are likewise subtle distinctions in the rounds' overall look.

Some of them have a dark and shiny black colour, while others beam with the colours of the woodland as well as have moss as well as lichen growing on their surfaces. Every one of them, nonetheless, has a mysterious and deep quality.

We find a tantalising hint of the stone spheres' beginnings in the variety of sizes and shapes that they are available in. Geological research has revealed that the spheres were made from a variety of stones, consisting of granodiorite, basalt, and sedimentary rock, amongst others. Because of this, the problem occurs regarding why the ancient artisans chose different kinds of stone for certain balls. Did the products have any kind of certain importance, or were they picked entirely based on exactly how easily available they were and also just how easily they could be made use of?

According to one institution of thought, the function or objective that the stones were supposed to serve might have affected the kind of stone that was picked for them. The long-lasting and strong granodiorite may have been chosen for balls that were planned to make it through the rigours of time as well as the elements, whilst the smooth and glossy basalt might have been assigned for ceremonial or aesthetic purposes.

When their larger cultural context is taken into account, the Stone Spheres show interesting affiliations to the ancient ideas and practises of Costa Rica's native peoples. These spheres are often uncovered at close distance to old villages, which offers support to the concept that they had an essential feature in the day-to-day life of these populaces.

Some researchers think that the spheres were utilised in astronomical monitoring, acting as markers or indications of certain beautiful events. Paperwork has revealed that there are positionings in between the balls as well as the locations of the sun, moon, or celebrities throughout the equinoxes and also solstices, which suggests that these individuals had a profound understanding of the cosmos.

The symbolic and spiritual relevance of the rounds likewise can not be overlooked and should be taken right into factor to consider. It's possible that the aboriginal occupants of Costa Rica saw these stones as icons of the Earth, the skies, or the cycles of life and death in their society. It's possible that they were items of respect, employed in routines as well as events as a way of communicating with the spirits that lived in the area.

While we guess about the possible interpretations and applications of the Stone Spheres, it is important that we additionally think about the tales and ideas that have been passed down via the generations. An extensive oral custom exists among the Diqus people, who are an indigenous area in Costa Rica. This tale connects the stones to old titans that formerly survived on the land as well as is passed down from generation to generation.

The Diqus titans were creatures of remarkable dimension and power who possessed profound knowledge as well as talents, according to ancient practices. They were in charge of the carving of the balls. It is informed that the giants worked vigilantly to develop the rounds, moulding them utilizing the toughness of their thoughts and also emotions.

These legends instil a feeling of awe and secret inside us, triggering us to contemplate the prospect of a period in human history that has been forgotten: a time when old giants, endowed with extraordinary skills, wandered the earth. Also if such stories may not make much feeling, they are a demonstration of the Stone Spheres' long-lasting appeal as well as of the human impulse to create misconceptions and tales about points that can not be discussed.

During the program of our investigation, we must recognise the ruthless efforts of modern excavators, scholars, and conservationists who have committed their lives to uncovering the enigmas bordering the Stone Spheres. Via their research study, they could clarify the cultural value of these strange artefacts as well as how they are interwoven with the natural as well as spiritual landscape of Costa Rica.

The spheres are currently protected from the effects of time and the tasks of human beings many thanks to the conservation efforts that have been placed right into location. A lot of the stones have been returned to their former positions, making it possible for guests to once more see their wonderful elegance and consider the tricks that the stones stand for.

As we come to the end of this chapter, let us review the sensible words of Mary Leakey, a popular archaeologist and historian from the United Kingdom. Leakey once mentioned, "The more one discovers, the much more one knows how little one recognizes." Stone Spheres of Costa Rica are a sobering reminder of the endless depths of human background and also the classic enigmas that remain to thrill our inquisitiveness. They were found in Costa Rica.

Let's go ahead with me, my readers, as we go further right into the centre of this globe of the rainforest, where ancient stones stand as guardians of neglected knowledge and also where the echoes of the previous telephone call out to us to check out the worlds of both myth and reality. The Stone Rounds are a demonstration of the determination of the spirit of query, a contact us to seek answers in one of the most unlikely of locations, as well as a reminder that the past is a bonanza of secrets just waiting to be figured out. All 3 of these points combine to make the Stone Spheres an effective icon.

CHAPTER 9: WERE THE NAZCA LINES AN ATTEMPT AT ASTRONOMICAL ART IN ANCIENT TIMES?

In the isolated desert plains of southerly Peru, a collection of enormous geoglyphs has been engraved into the very skin of the ground. These geoglyphs look like they were repainted on a large canvas of parchment, and also the planet itself appears like a huge canvas of parchment as it extends towards the horizon. These are the stunning and mysterious Nazca Lines, which are woven into the textile of time and area, and they welcome us to explore the tricks that they hang on both the celestial and the terrestrial aeroplanes.

We are welcomed with an unearthly environment as we make our means to the Nazca Plateau. It is a lonely expanse of sand as well as rock that extends for kilometres everywhere. It is in this barren wilderness that the Nazca Lines revive. These lines were carved right into the surface of the earth with a level of precision and also on a range that defies perception.

Think of a hummingbird with its wings spread out wide, prepared to fly, carved into the bottom of a desert with a wing period that is more than 300 feet long. Or it might be a crawler with very complicated information and an arm or leg period that has to do with 150 feet long. These gigantic sculptures, understood as geoglyphs, are not isolated abnormalities but rather belong to a widespread network of lines, forms, and forms that crisscross throughout the Nazca Plateau.

The sheer size and intricacy of the Nazca Lines are mind-boggling, which pleads the question that has attracted explorers and scholars for generations: Why were these geoglyphs constructed, as well as what message did they share with the old Nazca individuals?

An astronomical web link has been recommended by one concept, which is based upon the fact that the Nazca Lines correlate with particular holy sensations. The old Nazca society, which flourished between the years 200 BCE and 600 CE, had advanced expertise in the motions of the skies. This was evidenced by the existence of the Nazca Lines. It has been suggested that the geoglyphs they left behind may have been used as an astronomical schedule or as a means to track expensive occasions such as solstices as well as equinoxes.

When we consider the huge significance of the Nazca Lines, we can't yet be advised of the well-known number called the "Astronaut." Some individuals think that this humanoid number is a representation of an alien being-- an old astronaut that travelled to Earth eventually in our earth's background. This analysis is based on the number's extensive head as well as outstretched arms.

The principle of old astronauts as well as the duty they might have had in the growth of human civilization remains to ignite the interest of academics in addition to laypeople who want the topic. Could the Nazca Lines represent evidence of a conference with extraterrestrial entities, in addition to an indication of wonder as well as veneration for their transcendent visibility?

An additional concept claims that the Nazca Lines were connected to water routines and agricultural operations. Monitoring water resources was of miraculous significance to the inhabitants' capacity to endure in such a dry place as the Nazca Plateau. The geoglyphs might have been lined up with subsurface aquifers, riverbeds, or various other resources of water. They may have served as channels or pens to direct water circulation during the recurring yet crucial rainfalls that the region experiences.

It is possible that the Nazca civilisation, which was famous for its technical ability, made use of these geoglyphs as part of a complex system for transporting water to agricultural areas and maintaining the life of their populaces while staying in a desert atmosphere. According to this theory, the Nazca Lines are a demo of the creative thinking of ancient individuals as well as their ability to regulate the forces of nature.

Nevertheless, the more we consider these theories as well as examine the riddles bordering the Nazca Lines, the more we are confronted with the troubles that surround the formation of the lines. Just how was it possible for the Nazca civilisation, which did not have access to modern technology, to acquire such accuracy in their alignments and measurements when developing these massive geoglyphs?

The "stake as well as rope method" is a strategy that needs workers first noting out the preferred style with wooden stakes and after that using ropes to guide them while they get rid of the surface rocks as well as dirt to construct a geoglyph. This is just one of the theories that may be utilized to test the exercise of the "stake as well as rope technique." The precision of this system, on the other hand, raises additional questions about the Nazca individuals's understanding of geometry and measuring.

The practise of "dowsing," in which dowsing poles or other tools are used to discover subsurface water supplies, is yet one more theory that could discuss the formation of the Nazca Lines. These kinds of divinatory practices were popular in a whole lot of different ancient societies, as well as they could have been used to align the geoglyphs with water circulation patterns.

Throughout the program of our investigation into the Nazca Lines, we have been alerted of the perilous nature of these ancient antiques. The passage of time and the severe conditions of the desert atmosphere have both had an unfavourable influence on the geoglyphs. These old marvels are in danger of going away off the face of the earth as a result of disintegration, natural procedures, and the improvement of modern infrastructure.

Global and local organisations have teamed up to make an initiative to save as well as safeguard the Nazca Lines; yet, the problems that have to be gotten rid of are enormous. As we work in the direction of analyzing the mysteries of the Nazca Lines while additionally securing their long-lasting heritage, among the biggest challenges we have is striking a healthy and balanced equilibrium between the needs of conservation, which should take precedence over the imperatives of scientific research study as well as public access.

Allow us to beware of the words of the famous American archaeologist as well as traveller Hiram Bingham, who found the ancient Inca castle of Machu Picchu: "The look for lost cities as well as ancient civilizations is amongst the most remarkable of all human efforts." As we prepare to dive further right into the heart of the Nazca Lines, let us beware of these words. The Nazca Lines are an homage to this everlasting human endeavour; they are a testament to mankind's never-ending search for understanding, our respect for the tricks of the cosmos, and also our extensive web link to the material of background.

CHAPTER 10: THE COSMIC CONNECTION.

The Nazca Lines welcome us to investigate the possible planetary link that might have been the resource of their inspiration through the beautiful patterns as well as outstanding alignments that they include. We are drawn into a globe where the terrestrial and the incredible collide as we dive further into the centre of this secret. This is a realm in which the old Nazca people make every effort to connect the void between Earth and also deep space.

The lines etched into the Nazca Plateau are more than just geoglyphs; they are a witness to the intimate affinity that the Nazca civilization had with the incredible bodies that enhanced the night sky. The Nazca society lay in what is now the country of Peru. Not only did the sky influence awe in the Nazca individuals, but they additionally offered as a compass for their calendrical as well as agricultural practises, providing both a feeling of marvel and also a sense of objective.

The truth that the Nazca Lines are lined up with the solstices and equinoxes is probably one of the most distinctive expensive attributes that were put into them. These considerably huge incidents represented substantial turning points in the Nazca schedule, signalling the shifting of the periods in addition to the ideal times for sowing and harvesting. The meticulous arrangement of some geoglyphs, such as the Sun-Star, tips to the existence of an intentional style to denote these expensive events.

The Nazca human being had a clear obsession with the sunlight, which received much of the geoglyphs they produced. In their method of checking out the world, the sunlight, which gave both light and also life, was of miraculous value. It's feasible that the solar positioning of particular figures, like the Spiders and also the Sun-Star, acted as pens for solar incidents, highlighting the value of sunlight in their day-to-day life.

The moon was another vital heavenly body in Nazca astronomy, and also it was given a noticeable function in the technique. The phases and also cycles of the moon played a vital influence in determining when various agricultural procedures, most significantly the sowing of plants, happened. There is a possibility that specific geoglyphs, such as the Whale, were constructed to match lunar incidents. This would have enabled the Nazca people to check the moon as it moved via the evening sky.

The celestial links of the Nazca Lines go farther than just the solstices, equinoxes, as well as phases of the moon. It is assumed that some constellations' locations match the positionings of specific geoglyphs. It is believed that the Condor geoglyph is aligned with the constellation of the Southern Cross, which plays a crucial function in the Nazca folklore.

A better representation of the Nazca civilization's understanding of the rhythms as well as patterns of the night sky may be seen in the ceramics and textiles of that culture. Their creative work of art is decorated with elaborate pictures of different celestial worlds, constellations, and various other astrological aspects. These artefacts shed more light on the profound connection that the Nazca individuals had with the universe along with their wish to communicate this link through the art that they developed.

At the same time that we are checking out the cosmic web link of the Nazca Lines, we have to at the same time deal with the issues as well as secrets that are still out there. We are left amazed by the Nazca individuals' imaginative and technological capacity when we think about the large size as well as the excellence of these geoglyphs, which were sculpted right into the desert flooring with standard instruments. Exactly how were they able to achieve such incredible objectives without the support of contemporary innovation?

Because of their complex patterns and relatively random look, numerous geoglyphs resist uncomplicated categories due to the nature of their intended use. Were they just aesthetic productions that were inspired by the patterns of the evening skies, or did they have much more extensive symbolic implications that were only comprehended by the Nazca people?

The Nazca Lines, like the stars that inspired them, are a homage to the nonstop human search to connect with the cosmos as well as to find significance in the enormity of the cosmos. These lines were found in Peru in the early 20th century. They urge us to assess the vibrant relationship that exists between art, scientific research, and spirituality, as well as the night skies's timeless capacity to provoke admiration as well as questions in individuals.

Allow us to remember the words of the terrific astronomer Johannes Kepler as we prepare to endeavour further into the heart of this incredible enigma. Kepler once stated, "The diversity of the phenomena of nature is so terrific, as well as the prizes hidden in the heavens are so abundant, specifically so that the human mind shall never be lacking in fresh sustenance." The Nazca Lines function as a prompt suggestion that the splendour of deep space, both above as well as below, proceed to satiate our requirement for knowledge and our capacity for awe and wonder.

Join me, dear viewers, as we dive a lot more right into the intricate layouts and huge placements of the Nazca Lines in an initiative to uncover the cosmological mysteries that have continued for centuries. It is a trip that links the Planet and the celebrities, where the borders between the terrestrial and the holy blur into one mesmerising tapestry of human exploration and link. This is a journey that bridges the space between the Planet and the celebrities.

CHAPTER 11: THE SHROUD OF TURIN: A CONTROVERSIAL ANTIQUE

Within the sombre limits of the Sanctuary of Saint John the Baptist in Turin, Italy, a relic rests beneath a dimly lighted area. This antique is a linen fabric that has ordered the creative imagination and sustained enthusiastic disagreements for centuries. This enigmatic and also very disputed artefact is referred to as the Turin Shadow, and it is said to have been utilized as the textile that covered Jesus Christ's body during his funeral. As we discover deeper into the mysteries of this old relic, we find that we are being dragged into an intricate web of historical mysteries, scientific secrets, as well as spiritual enigmas that remain to perplex as well as charm us.

The Shadow of Turin, likewise called the Holy Shadow, is a rectangular item of linen fabric that is about 14 feet by 3.5 feet. It is said to have been utilized to wrap the body of Jesus Christ after his fatality. It is diligently woven in a herringbone pattern as well as carries the faint yet haunting image of a guy's face as well as upper body, both front as well as back. The pattern is herringbone.

The image seems that of a man who was tortured, with injuries that follow the description of Christ's crucifixion that is located in the Scriptures.

The power of the representation hits us like a tonne of blocks right away when we are standing here in the existence of this divine antique. It appears as if, from the depths of time, the tranquil yet deeply scarred face of a male who has endured great pain keeps an eye out at the world. The fact that the eyes are shut suggests that the individual has reached a state of calm rest, although the hands carry the wounds of nails and the side reveals the mark of a spear. This is evidence of the crucifixion that is recounted in the New Testament.

The course that the Shroud has taken via time is likewise shrouded in enigma. It is unidentified where it originated from, and the very first historical mention of it goes back to the 14th century, when it remained in the possession of a French knight called Geoffroi de Charny. On the other hand, its background before this is still a mystery, and some concepts claim it may have been in the possession of very early Christian groups.

The nature of the picture that is revealed on the Shroud is one of the variables that has triggered the most consternation among scholars. It does not show up to be a traditional painting or pigment, but rather what looks to be a photographic negative, which is a photo that was produced without using any type of imaginative processes that are currently recognised. The image seems the item of some sort of chemical or physical call between the fabric as well as the flesh that it had formerly enclosed. The bed linen itself displays no traces of colours or dyes; rather, it seems to be the consequence of this communication.

Due to its mysterious nature, the Shroud has been the subject of heated debates over its legitimacy. Sceptics describe the findings of scientific studies that have generated ambiguous outcomes as proof that the textile concerned is not the funeral shroud that Jesus Christ was covered in when he was laid to relax. The Shroud of Turin was subjected to radiocarbon testing in the last fifty per cent of the 20th century, and the results revealed that it belonged to the years 1260 CE to 1390 CE, which calls into question its web link to the time of Christ.

The Holy Shadow proceeds to evoke respect and devotion among all who see it. Scientists have been baffled by the image's thorough ins and outs, such as the scourge scars and also bloodstains, in addition to the unique top qualities of the image itself. The question of exactly how a mediaeval forger could have completed such a miraculous result stays unresolved, presuming that the record in inquiry is counterfeit in the first area.

The photo on the Shadow itself is something that individuals are fascinated by as well as wish to learn even more about. In the year 1898, an Italian digital photographer by the name of Secondo Pia caught the initial photo unfavourable of the Shadow, showing the creepy subtleties of the picture in clarity that had never been seen before. The photo negative illuminated the nuances of the photo, which made it possible for scholars to take a look at the Shroud's one-of-a-kind top qualities in even more information.

As we check out the picture on the Shadow in higher depth, our interest is consistently brought into the wounds that are visible on the remains. The bloodstains, which are dispersed in patterns that are suitable for the injuries tape-recorded in the Gospels, appear brownish because oxidation triggers them to turn that colour. According to historical records of crucifixion treatments in the ancient Roman era, the wounds triggered by the nails were positioned on the wrists instead of the hands of the target's hands.

The guidelines of gravity and anatomy are followed in the

depiction of the flow of blood from the nose in addition to the puncture hole in the side, which represents the spear drive. A combination of the photo's unique photo high qualities and the careful attention to anatomical information has left scientists baffled regarding exactly how it was generated in the first location.

The photo that is seen on the Shroud of Turin is said by some to have been generated by an extreme flash of radiant energy or radiation. According to this suggestion, which is also called the "Resurrection Occasion theory," the great power discharge that took place in combination with Christ's resurrection may have been in charge of imprinting his picture on the textile.

Other hypotheses propose that the formation of the image might have been the outcome of a chemical interaction between human liquids as well as the linen made use of in the experiment. Some individuals think that the picture was developed using a type of get-in-touch-photography, in which the body sent out radiation that interacted with the linen to leave a long-term impact on it. This theory has been produced by a few researchers.

The picture on the Shadow is also distinctive because it has a three-dimensional quality, which may be seen with more contemporary imaging techniques. To map the topography of the photo, researchers have utilized methods such as photogrammetry and also computerised evaluation. As a result, they have discovered a sensational deepness as well as uniformity that can not be represented using traditional kinds of creative expression.

When we consider the Shroud of Turin, we are drawn into the intersection of religion, clinical investigation, as well as the mission for historical truth. It is a relic that has caused researchers as well as believers to disagree, which brings into question our expertise of the old globe along with the limits of human comprehension.

We are reminded of the words of the thinker Albert Camus as we proceed with our examination right into the Shroud of Turin. Camus once claimed that to comprehend what is taking place worldwide, one has to relax from it now and then. The Shadow of Turin encourages us to step aside from the daily and also right into the outstanding, to consider what is inexplicable and also extensive on the planet around us, and also to do so with an open mind.

Join me, dear viewers, as we proceed our exploration into the centre of this controversial antique to resolve the riddle of the Shadow of Turin and the concerns it raises regarding faith, science, as well as the unresolved puzzles of human background. It is a trip that encourages us to look past the cloak of obscurity as well as right into the world of wonder and representation as we make our method through it.

CHAPTER 12: THE SECRET OF THE ENIGMA IS DISCLOSED

As we proceed with our investigation of the Shroud of Turin, we are led additionally as well as further right into the maze-like complexity of its secret. This old relic has been at the centre of a controversial debate for decades, and it has mesmerized both the hearts as well as imaginations of people who rely on its superordinary powers and also others who question them. Even with this, there are periodic flashes of understanding and enlightenment among the disagreements and also obscurity surrounding the Shadow; these glimpses of comprehension hint at the significant significance of the relic.

The image itself is among the most remarkable functions of the Shadow since it is a portrayal of a man being crucified that is so reasonable that it opposes the constraints of both time and creative capability. It is a picture that not only shows the psychological and physical distress that was experienced but also a sense of transcendence and peace. When a person passes away, their eyes appear to be looking beyond the domain of earth, which provides an idea to an extra spiritual and profound level.

The photo on the Shadow has been scrutinised by scientists utilizing a wide array of innovative strategies, tools, and innovations to determine its authenticity. In 1978, a team of well-informed people working under the auspices of the Shadow of Turin Research Study Project (STURP) executed a thorough analysis of the relic. Throughout their experiments, they made use of a range of strategies, consisting of photography, UV imaging, and also spectroscopy.

The image appeared to have a three-dimensional appearance, just one of the discoveries that triggered the best complication. Researchers from STURP utilized photogrammetry to construct precise topographic maps of the picture. These maps showed that the Shroud had the features of a genuine three-dimensional alleviation. This event contradicts what is considered to be conventional imaginative representation and also tips at a distinctive as well as mysterious treatment that was made use of to develop the picture.

The photo unfavourable high qualities of the image of the Shadow of Turin, which was discovered by Secondo Pia in the year 1898, proceed to provide intrigue. Since the photo can just be seen when seen in photo adverse, this has motivated some individuals to recommend that the Shadow may have been developed utilizing an early innovation for digital photography. This explanation has its very own unique set of concerns as well as problems.

The age of the Shroud of Turin is a subject that has been the subject of much controversy and conversation. The outcomes of radiocarbon dating done in the 1980s suggested that the Shadow was produced throughout the mediaeval duration, particularly between the years 1260 and 1390 CE. Believers who had intended to find a straight link to the time of Christ were left sensation discontented and also sceptical as an outcome of this conclusion.

Nonetheless, the integrity of the radiocarbon dating has been doubted by several scientists. Some academics argue that the Shadow may have been tainted with impurities over the training course of its background, which would affect the dating outcomes. The age of the Shroud has not been effectively established, and some professionals are asking for even more screening and investigation into the matter.

The Shroud of Turin has, in enhancement to the image itself, a variety of extra peculiar characteristics that need to be analyzed. Plant pollen and dust grains that were discovered on the fabric have provided some insight into the most likely trip that it had across both time and room. The examination of these fragments has resulted in the hypothesis that there is a connection to the Middle East, which provides trustworthiness to the concept that the Shadow might have been in the area of ancient Jerusalem at some time.

The bloodstains located on the Shroud have additionally been the subject of scrutiny by researchers. After studying the blood, scientists found the presence of bilirubin, a pigment that prevails in human blood and can be the result of damage or injury. The placement of the bloodstains on the Shadow of Turin is constant with the injuries that are videotaped in the Gospel narratives of Christ's crucifixion.

In the course of deciphering the puzzles surrounding the Shroud, we have bumped into an apparent contradiction. The relic opposes straightforward classification due to the extreme nature of its clinical qualities, distinctive look, and also substantial historical trip. It is a remnant that resists our understanding of deep space and the bounds of human knowledge, and it does so by straddling the line between confidence and factor.

The determination of the human search for meaning and a sense of transcendence is stood for by the Shroud of Turin as an icon. It is an antique that has influenced dedication as well as ideas for many years, a noticeable web link to a remote past that continues to arouse surprise and interest. For generations, people have been motivated to commit themselves to it and meditate on it.

As we proceed to examine the Turin Shadow, we are reminded words of the great mediaeval philosopher Thomas Aquinas, who stated, "To one who has confidence, no explanation is needed." To a person that does not have confidence, no explanation can be provided." The Shadow of Turin motivates us to assess the fantastic secrets of our faith and to open ourselves up to the idea that some things just can not be discussed.

My viewers, It is a journey that takes us to the side of discovery, where the mystery of the Shadow discloses itself in unforeseen ways, leaving us in awe at the complexities of the human experience that most of us share.

CHAPTER 13:
THE FANTASTIC PYRAMIDS OF GIZA AS ARCHITECTURAL MARVELS.

The Great Pyramids of Giza stand as towering sentinels of human resourcefulness in the middle of the limitless area of the Egyptian desert, where the golden sands expand as far as the eye can see. These mysterious as well as enforcing frameworks have been around for millennia, and they continue to keep the secrets of a bygone age secure under their watchful eyes. As we make our method even more right into the heart of these building wonders, we are reclaimed in time to a society that pushed the boundaries of what was believed to be possible.

The Great Pyramids of Giza stand as a homage to both the boldness of old Egypt's pharaohs as well as the unbelievable skill of the craftsmen who brought the pharaohs' dreams to fact. These pyramids were constructed around 4,000 years ago. These splendid holy places, called Khufu (or Cheops), Khafre, and Menkaure, represent the zenith of architectural accomplishment, as well as they have created individuals around the world to be in a state of nonstop awe.

The Great Pyramid of Khufu, the biggest and most well-known of the 3 pyramids, acts as the starting factor for our expedition of the world of the pyramids. As we get closer to its imposing limestone front, the size of the task that its home builders had to complete ends up being instantly evident to us. The Great Pyramid is a veritable titan of the Old World, standing at a remarkable height of around 481 feet (147 metres).

The pyramid was created with an incredible level of accuracy, which is nothing brief of impressive. The substantial rock pieces, some of which considered as much as 80 tonnes each, were extracted from quarries in the surrounding area as well as transferred with an amazing level of effectiveness. It is not recognized for specific just how these enormous rocks were relocated from one location to an additional; several of the theories that have been suggested consist of the exercise of sledges, canals, and a detailed network of ramps.

We are awestruck by the rigour with which the Great Pyramid's stones were set up as we stand in its darkness. The smooth appearance of the surface betrays the details of the interior structure, which is developed of blocks that fit with each other securely. The pyramid is made up of approximately 2.3 million individual stones, each of which was fastidiously put in to develop the unique tipped profile that has become associated with Egyptian pyramids.

The Great Pyramid is an architectural accomplishment in more methods than one, and also not only in its outside look. Its within is an intricate maze containing a puzzle of passages, rooms, as well as passages, every one of which was developed with such a degree of precision and purpose that it is challenging to explain. The huge coffin constructed from red granite that is housed in the centre area, which is additionally described as the King's

Chamber, is the spot where some individuals think Pharaoh Khufu was laid to rest.

The path that causes the King's Chamber is a constrained corridor that rises at a severe angle. This tunnel is referred to as the Ascending course. The old Egyptians' astronomical understanding is shown by the reality that this framework's measurements have been computed with such precision that it accompanies the celestial North Pole. Along with being just one of the most striking elements of the Great Pyramid, the Grand Gallery is a lofty flow that brings about the King's Chamber and is decorated with corbelled ceilings and huge granite beams.

As we venture deeper inside the Great Pyramid, we exist with the unresolved puzzle of exactly how it was constructed as well as why it was built. We have not been able to discover the accurate treatments that the ancient Egyptians made use of to move the substantial rocks and also put them in their appropriate settings. Various hypotheses have been proposed, some of which include using bars and counterweights, while others suggest the utilisation of a spiral ramp that may have ringed the perimeter of the pyramid.

The Great Pyramid's alignment with the cardinal points of the compass, along with its addition of specific astronomical estimations, has led some to presume that it offered not only as a spectacular mausoleum but also as a huge observatory. It is believed that the shafts that stretch from the King's Chamber to the outside of the pyramid had astronomical relevance since they provided a sight of particular stars and constellations.

When we direct our focus to the 2nd pyramid at Giza, which is called the Pyramid of Khafre, we are surprised by the distinctive features that it possesses. The mysterious Sphinx, a massive figure with the body of a lion and the head of a pharaoh, bases on either side of the pyramid of Khafre, which is just marginally smaller than that of Khufu. The complicated at Giza provided an included air of mystique through the presence of the Sphinx, with its expression that can not be figured out as well as its air of old-time expertise.

The 3rd as well as the tiniest pyramid at Giza, that of Pharaoh Menkaure, reveals its unique building wonders. The truth that it is enhanced with the antiques of polished granite casing rocks is evidence of the high-end as well as craftsmanship of ancient Egypt. The interior of the pyramid of Menkaure screens, just like the interiors of the pyramids that came before it, is a complex network of chambers and hallways.

We are advised of the words of the old historian Herodotus as we stand here in the middle of these building marvels: "Concerning Egypt itself, I shall extend my statements to a fantastic length since there is no country that has so many wonders." The Great Pyramids of Giza are undoubtedly wonders that could hold the attention of people of all ages throughout their existence.

The Pyramids have been a resource of unlimited intrigue as well as investigation ever before given that they were initially uncovered. Just how did the ancient Egyptians construct their buildings with such precision and percentage to the area they inhabited? Where did the concept for the layout come from, and also what was the main feature of these massive structures? There is a huge selection of theories, varying from those that are engineering-focused and pragmatic to those that are magical as well as cosmic.

There is a concept that recommends the pyramids were constructed to function as monumental tombs for pharaohs. These tombs were meant to house the pharaohs' physical remains as well as make it much easier for them to travel to immortality.

This theory is supported by the complex hieroglyphic inscriptions and funerary rites discovered within the pyramids. Nevertheless, there is still a great deal of controversy around the specifics of the pharaohs' beliefs and the rituals that were included with the building and construction of the pyramids.

There is additionally the possibility that the pyramids had a cosmological significance. According to this theory, the pyramids lined up with huge incidents as well as functioned as building representations of the pharaoh's magnificent authority. This concept is sustained by the accuracy of their building, which straightens them with the primary factors, in addition to the fact that they are associated with astronomical events.

The orientation of the pyramids, in which each side is oriented to one of the four cardinal instructions (north, south, east, and also west), supplies an additional layer of implying to the structures. This meticulous placement not only illustrates the old Egyptians' reverence for the order of the cosmos but also their decision to maintain the pharaoh's rule as well as preserve peace in immortality.

Through proceeded research as well as excavation, the Great Pyramids of Giza proceeded to disclose the secrets that had been hidden inside them. Recent explorations, such as secret chambers and tunnels, offer tantalising sights into the details of these structures as well as the opportunity for future disclosures. Current explorations consist of concealed chambers and passages.

As we come to the end of our tour of the Great Pyramids of Giza, we are loaded with a tremendous feeling of wonder and veneration for these ancient frameworks. These building marvels are a monolith of human ambition, inspiration, and also the ongoing look for immortality. They were considered as well as developed by a society that existed countless years back.

Going further, as we continue to go deeper into the centre of these ageless frameworks to decipher the tricks they harbour and the stories they recite from the midst of history. This is a trip that goes beyond the confines of time as well as area, taking us on a trip that forces us to assess the enduring tradition of the ancient Egyptians as well as the infinite opportunities of what human beings can do.

CHAPTER 14:
THE ENGINEERS
OF INFINITY

As we check out much more into the mystery bordering the Great Pyramids of Giza, we locate that as we do so, we can peek not just at the big stone structures, but also right into the lives and minds of the designers and labourers that was in charge of bringing these huge marvels into fact. The pyramids are a peaceful witness to the imagination, devotion, as well as stubborn vision of the people who were responsible for shaping them. They stand as eternal sentinels in the desert.

The building of the Great Pyramids is evidence of the mindful preparation and organisation that characterised the world of ancient Egypt, as seen by the reality that they were able to be constructed. A wonderful command of maths, engineering, and architecture was shown by the architects as well as engineers who were accountable for the conception of these large buildings. Their knowledge of geometry, checking, as well as the auto mechanics of constructing frameworks, allowed them to develop and construct these monuments with a level of precision that is rather astonishing.

The identity of the master builder who was in charge of the construction of the Great Pyramid of Khufu is still unknown. Inscriptions and also historical resources, on the other hand, offer the impact that the part played by the architect was of the highest value. They were tasked with translating the pharaoh's vision into architectural reality while also managing every facet of the building process.

The old builders were faced with several significant barriers, one of the most significant of which was the transportation of the large stone obstructs from the quarries to the pyramid's construction site. Stones of enormous size, some of which weighed as long as 80 tonnes each, were extracted from quarries that were situated a few kilometres away. The extraordinary task of logistics required to transfer these huge rocks across the arid landscape continues to be a subject of intrigue and examination.

To describe how the stone blocks were relocated, numerous explanations and theories have existed. Some people advise utilizing sledges and lubrication, either with water or veggie issues, to minimize the amount of friction. Others propose the advancement of causeways or rails, while one more hypothesis posits the employment of counterweights as well as a winding device to raise the stones into location.

We are reminded of the amazing engineering expertise of the old Egyptians whenever we consider the way by which these huge rocks were moved and raised. To achieve their enthusiastic goal, the old Egyptians made use of the power of human work combined with the legislations of physics to build the pyramids that stand as a testimony to their capacity to victory over challenges that seemed insurmountable.

The workforce that was utilized in the construction of the pyramids was huge and also comprised people from various backgrounds. It was composed of expert labourers, architects, as well as craftsmen who were well-familiarized with the procedures and fundamentals of pyramid construction. Old Egyptian human can effectively arrange their labour and subordinate it to the centralised authority of the pharaoh is proof of the society's prowess in administrative matters.

It is a common mistaken belief that the people who functioned in developing the pyramids were slaves; nevertheless, this is not the situation. Instead, they were divided up into job groups that were referred to as "gangs," as well as each of these gangs was accountable for a certain element of the building and construction process. As a demo of the pharaoh's obligation to the workers' wellness, he ensured they had access to food, housing, and clinical therapy.

The tools that the labourers used were straightforward yet did the task well. The principal tools that were used for quarrying as well as shaping the stone blocks were copper blades, rock hammers, as well as wood sledges. The capacity and experience of the staff members are shown by the precision with which these tools were employed, along with the efficiency of the workforce.

The structure of the pyramids was not a spontaneous endeavour; rather, it was a project that was carefully prepared and performed over several decades. This task needed the control of a large number of workers. The sophisticated social as well as management institutions of ancient Egypt are reflected in the reliable organisation and administration of such an enormous task.

The objective, as well as the definition of the labyrinthine interior tunnels as well as chambers of the pyramids, is one of the mysteries that have continued for centuries since their production. Some of the areas were utilized as burial places for pharaohs and stored funeral artefacts, it is feasible that other chambers had ceremonial or symbolic objectives. There is still much room for guesswork and analysis about the importance of each of these rooms.

The ancient Egyptians' sentences worrying the immortality and the pharaoh's magnificent setting were delicately intertwined with the process whereby the pyramids were constructed. In addition to their use as burial places, the pyramids were additionally believed to have contributed to the pharaoh's flow to immortality. The pharaoh's divine power as well as the unbroken family tree of the Egyptian state were both emphasised by the interment rites as well as inscriptions that were situated within the pyramids.

When we take into consideration the labourers as well as architects who committed their lives to the building of the Great Pyramids, we are brought back to the enduring legacy that their success has left behind. Their unwavering dedication to their art, their unshakable trust fund in the pharaoh's vision, as well as their capability to harness the forces of nature are an homage to the loftiest accomplishments of human endeavour.

The pyramids remain to provide attraction as well as respect for individuals, and also they function as a web link that extends the gulf of time to bring us closer to the world of classical times and the tricks it still harbours. They are a demonstration of the infinite possibility of human imagination and also the incessant requirement to make one's mark on the textile of history.

Occur with me, dear viewers, as we continue our exploration of the world of the pyramid home builders as well as attempt to find out the secrets of the architectural wonders they produced and also the heritage they left behind. It is a trip that permits us to appreciate the long-lasting power of human vision and partnership while additionally allowing us to place ourselves in the shoes of individuals who constructed the ancient world.

CHAPTER 15: THE EASTER ISLAND MOAI: GIANTS OR ENGINEERING MARVELS?

The enigmatic Moai of Easter Island may be discovered on a remote island in the middle of the area of the South Pacific Sea, not much from where the perspective satisfies the infinite blue. This island is the residence of one of the most mysterious and amazing wonders of human workmanship and also is called Easter Island. These massive stone statuaries have given fascination to travellers, archaeologists, and daydreamers for hundreds of years as a result of their imperious presence and stoic watchfulness. As we established out on a trip to discover the secrets surrounding the Moai, we located ourselves moved to an island that was as soon as home to titans or technical wonders.

Located in the centre of the Pacific Ocean, some 3,700 kilometres (2,300 miles) west of the coast of Chile, a little speck of land referred to as Easter Island is home to a populace of indigenous Polynesians that call it Rapa Nui. The truth that it is cut off from the rest of the globe by a massive nautical expanse offers an air of intrigue to the story it informs. The island itself is a volcanic wonder, as well as its rocky topography, has been carved by geological processes over the program of centuries.

An old civilisation once flourished on this remote island, as revealed by the Moai, which are monolithic stone titans that stand as guards of that culture. These statuaries, which were hewn from the volcanic rock of the island, work as both instances of the engineering expertise of people and also as symbols of a mysterious civilisation that was as soon as thriving but which at some point underwent a dreadful failure.

The Moai be available in a range of sizes, with the biggest getting to heights of over 30 feet (9 metres) and weighing as high as 80 tonnes. Since their substantial size, there has been an endless conversation concerning just how these gigantic statuaries were relocated to as well as set up on a hard-to-reach island with a restricted supply of products. Their magnitude alone is remarkably sufficient to motivate wonder.

When we stand before the Moai, we are shocked not simply by their dimension but also by the degree of information that was placed into their features. Each sculpture is a unique portrayal, with its own set of distinctive facial qualities and a distinctly crafted carving technique. The major functions as well as huge foreheads of the Moai are framed by topknots, also understood as "pukao," which are carved from various sorts of rock than the remainder of their heads.

The Moai were formed from volcanic tuff, which is a rock that is soft and somewhat permeable and may be found in the quarries of Rano Raraku, which is a volcanic crater on the island. It took a great deal of effort as well as cautious attention to information to carve the Moai out of the rock. The number was carved right into the rock by damaging it with rock devices like lava adzes as well as various other similar carries. Progressively, the shapes of the number within the rock ended up being visible.

The accuracy with which the Moai were carved is probably among the most impressive aspects of these old statuaries. The ancient island's craftsmen were very skilled and imaginative, as seen by the quantity of information that was carved into their facial functions, which consisted of every little thing from the eyes and noses to the lips. The careful workmanship offers the impression that each figure has some extensive social as well as spiritual definition connected to it.

The even more we believe about how these substantial rock numbers were moved from the quarries of Rano Raraku to their supreme relaxing places along the shore of Easter Island, the more mysterious the Moai seem. There is a wide variety of speculation on the settings of transportation, including the utilisation of logs and also rolling, as well as the exercise of a rocking motion described as "walking.".

In particular, the "strolling" concept has been attracting a great deal of interest. It seems to indicate that the Moai were moved by guiding them to and fro in a zigzag pattern while being supported by stone ramps as well as systems. This lengthy procedure demanded a concerted effort from the group overall, in addition to exact timing, to avoid the sculptures from dropping over.

Nonetheless, moving the Moai was just a tiny section of the enormous task that required to be finished. Equally hard was the process of putting up these huge numbers right into their last positionings, which were often located atop ceremonial platforms called "ahu." It is feasible that additional ramps and also bars were utilised as components of the procedure to increase the Moai into an upright position.

Recurring research studies as well as discussions centre on the question of whether or not the Moai play a considerable role in the cultural practices of Rapa Nui. According to a couple of colleges of thought, the sculptures concerned were meant to personify valued ancestors or influential tribal leaders as well as work as avenues between the material world and the spiritual one. It is asserted that the topknots, additionally called pukao, show the way the hair of high-status persons is tied back.

The construction of the Moai was followed by a series of complicated ceremonies as well as ceremonies, which included the process of sculpting the sculptures, moving them, and lastly positioning them on the ahu where they were to be completely presented. These ceremonies possibly played a substantial part in the social as well as spiritual lives of the individuals who survived the island. They offered to strengthen the connection between the living and also the spirits of the forefathers.

A phase in Easter Island's history that is both troubling and mysterious is the fall of the Moai culture, which was qualified by the devastation of sculptures and also the abandoning of ahu. It has been hypothesised that the eco-friendly collapse of the island was induced by human activity, especially deforestation and the exhaustion of the island's all-natural sources.

The tale of the Moai remains to enthral people's imaginations as well as inspire them to seek even more information. It is a monolith to the everlasting human yearning for innovative expression along with the human capability to grasp the obstacles of design. The Moai are greater than just sculptures; they are depictions of an ancient society's originality and resiliency when faced with ecological modification and also the challenges of living in seclusion.

We are reminded of the words of the explorer Thor Heyerdahl, who saw Easter Island in the middle of the 20th century: "Rapa

Nui ought to remind all of us that our planet needs extra research study as well as conservation, not a lot more tourists." As we stand right here in the existence of these towering stone giants, we are reminded of those words.

Dear reader, as we continue our expedition of the secrets that border Easter Island. Our objective is to find out the facts behind the Moai sculptures and the stories that these statues need to tell concerning a society that once flourished in magnificent isolation. This is a trip that encourages us to reflect on the ever-present pressure of human creation along with the profound link that exists between society and the all-natural globe.

CHAPTER 16: THE RONGORONGO MANUSCRIPT: UNDERSTANDING THE ENIGMA

As we proceed with our research study of Easter Island, we uncover that we are being dragged further into the Rongorongo script, which is at the centre of the island's secret. The Rongorongo script is a hieroglyphic writing system that can be discovered on Easter Island. It is commonly considered one of the most challenging as well as puzzling to check out composing systems in the world. Scientists and linguists continue to be astonished by the old civilization of the island, which is suggested by the presence of this artefact, which recommends a high degree of sophistication and intricacy within that civilisation.

The Rongorongo script is made up of glyphs that are sculpted onto various other artefacts and wood tablet computers. These glyphs are used to create the language. The real glyphs are complex and differ, comprising a variety of signs that reveal animal as well as human personalities, vegetation, geometric structures, and abstract patterns. These symbols might be located inside the glyphs. The glyphs are outlined in rows as well as being checked out from delegated right when the script is being checked out.

There is still a great deal of confusion about where the Rongorongo manuscript came from. It is taken into consideration to have come from separately on Easter Island because there is no indication of external impact or interaction with various other people that might discuss its existence. This results from the fact that there is no proof of its presence. It is thought that the writing has been in use for several centuries, which was first created on wood tablet computers called "kohau rongorongo."

The reality that a translated translation of the Rongorongo script does not exist is one of the qualities of the composing system that is one of the most confusing. Linguists, chroniclers, and scholars have invested years attempting to analyze the definition of the writing, but they have not been successful. The complexity of the icons and the lack of a recognized bilingual message have made deciphering them a very uphill struggle.

According to one college of the idea, the manuscript could be an example of a kind of proto-writing, which is specified as a system of symbols that communicate definitions in the absence of a recognized grammar or syntax. According to this theory, the script may have been used as a mnemonic gadget or as a method for preserving details, much as just how early writing systems were made use of in various other ancient societies.

The deciphering of particular icons has become a tough as well as complicated task. While a few of the symbols seem to portray recognisable points like birds, fish, or human beings, others remain strange and abstract. Comprehending the syntax and the context in which these symbols were utilized is the hard part of the problem.

The decipherment initiatives are made a lot harder by the

minimal variety of Rongorongo artefacts that have survived. As they were in touch with European explorers and settlers, most of the wood tablets and other things that birthed the writing were either lost or damaged. It is challenging to compile a comprehensive corpus for research study because there are only a select couple of Rongorongo artefacts that have made it through into the modern day.

One of the appealing qualities of the Rongorongo script is the concept that it may provide clues to the background, culture, as well as folklore of the island. This is one of one of the most fascinating parts of the writing. Researchers have hypothesised that the writing might consist of documents of genealogy, understanding of navigation, or rites connected with ritualistic practises. These opportunities are still just suppositions, nonetheless, since there is no known means to analyze the significance of the writing.

The particular biological as well as cultural restrictions presented by Easter Island's remote place add to the Rongorongo script's appearance as a writing system. It is feasible that the locals of the island, who were recognized as the Rapa Nui and also lived in an atmosphere that was vibrant and had few resources, were in charge of the invention and usage of the manuscript. The enigmas bordering Easter Island's history and the fate of its long-lost civilisation remain to hold a solid hang on individuals's creativities.

Researchers have tried a variety of various approaches in their initiative to interpret the Rongorongo script. The meaning of the manuscript has been checked out with relative research with lots of other Polynesian languages and also signs in an initiative to find possible linguistic affiliations that may clarify its importance. On top of that, cutting-edge computer techniques and computational grammar were made use of to do an examination right into the connections and patterns consisted of within the glyphs.

Nevertheless, even with every one of these attempts, the Rongorongo script is still an enigma; it is a puzzle that has not been addressed, and it tortures scholars and linguists with its difficulty and evasiveness. The indecipherability of the writing ignites our curiosity as well as encourages conjecture, which consequently obliges us to think of the consistent enigmas of the human world and interaction.

As we draw to a close on our examination of the Rongorongo manuscript, we are entrusted with a feeling that is equal components curiosity as humility. The script is a moving instance of the breadth and deepness of human creativity, along with the relentless search for details and opportunities for expression. It acts as a reminder that the human spirit is durable, even when faced with strange riddles, as well as will certainly remain to function towards analyzing the mysteries of the past.

Go along with me, dear viewers, as we proceed our expedition of the globe of Easter Island in an initiative to understand the enigmas of the Rongorongo alphabet as well as the prospective tales that it might contain. This is a trip that encourages us to acknowledge the ever-present appeal of the undiscovered and also to value the unlimited possibilities for human expedition and analysis.

CHAPTER 17: THE ENIGMA OF THE CRYSTAL SKULLS: ANCIENT ALIENS OR HOAX?

The mysterious crystal skulls are kept in the poorly lit rooms of museums and exclusive collections all around the globe. They are components of a collection of mesmerising artefacts that are waiting for our interest. These skull-shaped sculptures, which are sculpted from either milky-white or clear quartz crystal, have mesmerized the minds of followers, sceptics, and academics alike. They are the subject of conundrum, conjecture, and intrigue, as well as their histories are masked in obscurity. Are these crystal heads artefacts from a long-lost and technologically sophisticated culture, websites to the knowledge of space beings, or cunning frauds meant to amuse as well as confuse?

According to the stories, the tale of the crystal skulls might be mapped back to the distant past when they were initially uncovered. Old civilizations such as the Mayans and others are credited with the development of these transparent heads, which some records claim day back thousands of years. It is assumed that the Mayans, who were famous for their accomplishments in astronomy as well as math, carved these heads with careful accuracy, imbuing them with wonderful powers and cosmic wisdom while doing so.

The earliest circumstances of a crystal head have been documented in modern times days back to the latter fifty percent of the 19th century. In 1924, the intrepid tourist and explorer Anna Mitchell-Hedges stated that she had found a crystal head in the middle of the damages of the Mayan city of Lubaantun in Belize, which is situated in Central America. Her story, which was supported by dazzling summaries of the find, was greatly in charge of catapulting the crystal skulls into the sphere of preferred inquisitiveness.

The crystal skull that came from Anna Mitchell-Hedges, often referred to as the "Mitchell-Hedges Head," is an impressive instance of skilled craftsmanship. It is made from a solitary piece of quartz crystal and has detailed components, such as a jawbone that can be gotten rid of and changed to offer the artefact a creepy as well as realistic appearance. The transparent high quality of the skull adds to its air of enigma by making it possible for light to dance and refract inside the crystallised recesses of the item.

The Mitchell-Hedges Skull, in addition to the credibility of various other crystal skulls, has been the emphasis of a lot of conversation and also scepticism throughout the years. Some individuals believe that old people would not have had the technological knowledge necessary to carve such intricate kinds out of quartz crystal considering that it would certainly have been too tough for them to do so. They also mention that there is no documented historical proof that can be used to link crystal skulls to certain ancient cultures.

On the other hand, several who believe in the existence of crystal skulls suggest that the art and modern technology of old individuals were much a lot more established than it is now because of the existence of these skulls. They argue that the skulls might have been used as stores of spiritual or cosmological expertise, which consisted of within the crystalline matrix of the skulls. Some people believe that the skulls were provided to human beings by unusual entities as presents and that they had the secrets to accessing buried wisdom.

The rising availability of crystal heads over the 21st and 20th centuries has added to the aura's level of obscurity. Throughout the globe, several crystal skulls, both ancient and much more recent in age, have been found in different places. Others of these skulls have been related to New Age activities as well as cases of having mythological capacities, while others have been linked to indigenous peoples as well as the spiritual customs that they practice.

The results of scientific research on crystal skulls have revealed some fascinating new information. Scientists have utilised strategies like as spectroscopy and electron microscopy to examine the composition of the heads along with the artistry that entered into making them. The findings have shown that numerous crystal skulls are built from natural quartz crystal, and there is no sign that they were fabricated utilizing modern-day tools or methods.

The supposed capability of crystal heads to both send as well as amplify energy is one of the lot more complicated attributes of these artefacts. In the existence of crystal skulls, some people declare to have had visions, been healed, or experienced increased degrees of understanding. The reality that these assertions are impossible and unscientific to confirm adds to the secret bordering the artefacts, which even raises their allure.

The scientific community is still divided on the question of where the crystal heads came from and what their importance is. Sceptics argue that crystal skulls are products of modern times, thoroughly made to appear like old artefacts to make use of the credulity of enthusiasts and connoisseurs. As evidence of the questionable authenticity of the skulls, they refer to the lack of provenance details and videotaped histories for many of the artefacts.

Others, on the other hand, have an open mind and urge that crystal heads go through strenuous scientific evaluation while also valuing the secrets that border them. They compete that throughout the history of human civilisation, there are numerous instances of remarkable workmanship as well as profound understanding that can not be discussed using extra typical approaches.

Crystal heads, with their mysterious appeal and transcendent appeal, proceed to be products that amaze and astound individuals. They are symbols of the eternal human yearning for understanding, mystery, and a connection to forces that extend beyond the everyday. Whether they are artefacts from a long-lost and also technically advanced society, the outcome of human wizards, or the outcome of shrewd scams, the crystal heads serve as a reminder of the endless capacity that exists inside the human creative imagination and creative capacity.

The words of Carl Sagan come to mind when we absorb the gleaming artefacts that surround us at this actual minute: "The absence of evidence is not proof of absence." The crystal heads encourage us to review the enigmas of the past, the untouched areas of the universes, as well as the eternal attraction of things that can not be discussed.

As we dig much more right into the secret surrounding the crystal heads. Together, we will certainly attempt to decipher the stories that the crystal skulls tell and the troubles that they cause the nature of human knowledge and the limitations of believing. It is a voyage into the domain of the weird and also the unexplained, where ancient secrets and modern-day scepticism merge in a dance of interest and marvel. This is a trip into the world of the unusual and also the inexplicable.

CHAPTER 18: THE CURSE OF THE CRYSTAL SKULLS

The world of crystal heads is not only a realm of mystical starts and interesting artefacts but also a phase for the drama of intrigue, idea, and conjecture. Since the crystal skulls are stated to have been created by old people, this is. The myths and tales that border these entrancing items frequently enter into the realms of the superordinary, spinning stories of curses, riddles, and mythological abilities that have fallen upon people who have entered into contact with these artefacts. These tales are said to have a mesmerising effect on those who hear them.

The Mitchell-Hedges Head, which was found by Anna Mitchell-Hedges in the damages of Lubaantun, is likely the crystal skull got in touch with the concept of a curse being connected with certain crystal skulls. Anna Mitchell-Hedges is claimed to have claimed that the head brought her both good luck as well as tragedy, which is supported by the accounts. She chatted not only about its supposed abilities to treat and forecast the future but also about the adversities and bad luck that fell upon any individual who risked strolling into its middle.

The Mitchell-Hedges Skull has established a notoriety for being an omen of misery, which has become an essential element of its backstory. The secret that borders this particular crystal skull was fanned by stories of calamities, fatalities, as well as various other regrettable occasions that were linked with the proprietors of the skull. Sceptics think that these sorts of events are the outcome of coincidence or superstitious notions.

There have been accounts of misfortune connected to various other crystal heads that are similar to those informed regarding this. After buying a crystal head, several owners and collection agencies have asserted to have experienced a string of misfortunes, personal obstacles, or other weird cases in their lives. These stories often muddy the waters between truth and tale, making it hard to determine where belief and also scepticism end and start.

These artefacts are considered treasuries of old wisdom and energy, according to among the hypotheses that have been installed relating to the crystal heads' supposed evil-minded influence. Heads might have the possibility to amplify as well as transfer energy, according to proponents of this hypothesis. This power, if abused or misunderstood, might cause unwanted consequences. They argue that the concept of a curse might have originated from the incident of these results.

It is difficult to disregard the power of pointers and the capacity of humans to produce their own self-fulfilling prophesies while talking about issues relating to ideas and the mythological. Those who are persuaded of the existence of the curse may blame damaging incidents on the crystal heads, which strengthens their confidence in the crystal heads' capacity to apply a bad effect.

On the other hand, several who believe crystal heads have some kind of restorative or spiritual meaning contend that by interacting with them in an open-minded and wholehearted fashion, one might experience a shift in the direction of much more favourable energy and also an extra transformative state. They suggest that the skulls may be used as tools for personal advancement, meditation, and also the extension of one's awareness.

The influence of belief, whether it be in a curse or the transformational possibility of crystal heads, highlights the intricacy of the human mind as well as its communication with things that are mysterious as well as remarkable. It throws into question the basis of belief, the function of symbols, and also the ever-present allure of the unidentified.

The concept that crystal skulls are in some means connected to a curse is consulted with scepticism and ridiculed as an item of superstition or sheer incident, according to a scientific and sceptical factor of view. Sceptics contend that connecting unfavourable occurrences to the skulls is an instance of a classic occurrence of confirmation prejudice, which occurs when a person selectively focuses on events that match with their existing sights.

The mystery bordering the crystal skulls, with every one of its confounding layers of idea, scepticism, and unanswered questions, urges us to check out the limitations of human vision as well as understanding. It compels us to consider the methods by which meaning, routine, and the power of the mind all add to the development of our experiences and beliefs.

As we proceed to dive deeper into the realm of crystal heads, we are met with extensive communication between believing and scepticism, as well as between the mystical as well as the rational. The crystal skulls are more than simply motionless things; they are home windows into the human mind, reflecting our relentless search for enigma, definition, and connection to pressures that are past our understanding.

Join me, dear visitor, as we check out the misconceptions and tales that have woven themselves into the material of the crystal heads as we make our way through the labyrinthine worlds of idea as well as scepticism and the globes of the crystal skulls. This is a voyage that urges us to consider the restrictions of reality and misconception, along with valuing the enduring power of human analysis and imagination.

CHAPTER 19: THE PIRI REIS MAP: DO WE HAVE PROOF OF LONG-LOST CIVILIZATIONS?

An artefact that has for ages attracted the imaginations of chroniclers, travellers, as well as conspiracy theory philosophers may be found concealed in the shadowy spaces as well as crannies of the Topkapi Palace Museum in Istanbul. This gem is concealed from the view of those who only pay the museum a passing see. It is a fragmented plan of the globe called the Piri Reis Map, and also it supplies a gateway to the marvels of the past while additionally increasing uncertainties about the understanding and expeditions of old people.

The amazing life of Admiral Piri Reis, an Ottoman sailor and also cartographer, is where the tale of the Piri Reis Map starts. This event occurs in the early 16th century. In 1470, Piri Reis was birthed in the busy port city of Gallipoli, which was known for its maritime profession at the time. He would certainly take the place to be renowned for his abilities in the fields of navigation and mapping. As a result of his most well-known book, the Kitab-i Bahriye (likewise called the Publication of Navigating), he is now taken into consideration as one of the most established travellers in history.

The Kitab-i Bahriye was a comprehensive recommendation for navigation as well as seamanship that ended in 1521. It was based on Piri Reis's considerable expertise in the Mediterranean and other areas past it. It had comprehensive maps and graphs, a few of which were based on the work of earlier explorers and cartographers. It was a demo of the Footrest Empire's long-lasting dedication to aquatic society.

The map in the Kitab-e Bahriye that is now referred to as the Piri Reis Map is thought to be the most popular of every map in the book. A partial piece of parchment determining approximately 90 by 60 centimetres contains this map that was attracted in the year 1513. Its picture of the globe, a world that tests our knowledge of background and exploration, is not just essential due to its age but likewise because of how it portrays the globe.

The Piri Reis Map stands apart from various other works of cartography developed throughout that period for several reasons. The representation of the New Globe, particularly the eastern coastline of South America as well as the western shore of Africa, is the first as well as most vital element of this job. These locations are revealed with an impressive degree of detail, including coastlines that cling to life as well as recognisable geographical qualities.

The fact that the map's origins remain maintained to date throughout several centuries by sailors and a secret is just one of its defining features. Piri Reis stated that he based his map on a collection of previous charts, some of which went back to the moment of Alexander the Great and also old worlds such as Egypt as well as Greece. Piri Reis's claim was based on the reality that he was the creator of the map. He declared that these products had been produced and maintained to date throughout several centuries by sailors as well as academics.

The topic of exactly how Piri Reis may have had accessibility to maps that predate the European exploration of the New World by Christopher Columbus in 1492 has been one that has interested historians and scientists for ages. Is it feasible that the Piri Reis Map consists of evidence of long-vanished civilizations or profound expertise from ancient times?

There is a notion that claims the maps that Piri Reis used might have been part of the famous Library of Alexandria. The Library of Alexandria was among one of the most popular expertise centres in the old globe. It is reported that a variety of disasters that occurred during antiquity brought about the destruction of the library, which was renowned for its substantial collection of scrolls and writings. If the maps did in reality originate from Alexandria, then the reality that they have been maintained for so long is a fascinating historical anomaly.

There is also the possibility that the Piri Reis Map was obtained from previous maps that prevailed among old sailors and also navigators. This is just one of the much more current theories on the origins of the map. These maps can have been passed on with the centuries, as a result preserving knowledge of the location and also expeditions that being successful worlds failed to remember or lost.

The accuracy of the portrayal of the New Globe that is seen on the Piri Reis Map is something that remains a subject of intrigue as well as disagreement. Some individuals argue that the map's representation of the South American coast, with every one of its bays as well as rivers, indicates a level of understanding that can not have been gotten simply from observation from a ship. They say this because the map shows rivers as well as bays. Some individuals think that Piri Reis may have assembled the map that we have today by making use of details from a range of various sources.

Additionally, the Piri Reis Map has a variety of mystical works and symbols that leave specialists scraping their heads. It appears that some of these inscriptions are composed in Arabic, while others are composed in what seems an antiquated kind of writing. The analysis of these inscriptions is still up for discussion, with some hypothesizing that they provide guidelines as to the beginnings and resources of the map in inquiry.

The Piri Reis Map was given newfound attention in the 20th century as a result of the advancement of various technologies. In the year 1960, the map was taken a looked at in wonderful detail making use of a selection of techniques, such as spectroscopy and infrared imaging. These evaluations discovered previously unidentified attributes and marks on the paper, which assisted in offering more understanding of the things' history and provenance.

On the map, among the shocking explorations was that there existed a network of going across lines and also grid patterns. This was among the grid patterns. Some academics think that these lines might have been made use of as a kind of latitude and longitude grid, which would need an extensive grasp of mapping as well as navigating on the part of individuals that drew them.

Also in the 21st century, individuals proceed to be attracted by as well as have strong opinions on the Piri Reis Map. Others continue to maintain their scepticism as well as search for various other possible theories as to where the map originated from, while others remain to examine the opportunities of long-lost human beings or old resources of information.

As we contemplate the unknowns surrounding the Piri Reis Map, we are brought in person with the unintelligible midsts of human curiosity in addition to the relentless requirement to discover new things as well as broaden our horizons. The map urges us to check out the idea that our knowledge of history and civilisation may be more complex as well as intertwined than we presently think it to be.

Join me, dear reader, as we continue our exploration of the globe shown on the Piri Reis Map. Our goal is to uncover the responses to the problems it elevates regarding the far-off past and the potential for unknown info to impact our perspective of the universe. It is a voyage that urges us to appreciate the long-lasting pressure of historical query and discovery as well as to accept the invitation to embrace the mysterious.

CHAPTER 20: WHAT KEYS DOES THE ORONTIUS FINAEUS MAP HOLD RELATING TO ANTARCTICA?

As we make our way even more right into the history of strange cartography, we uncover that we are pulled to one more map that provides a challenge to our understanding of ancient knowledge and exploration. This map is called the Orontius Finaeus Map. This map, which may be located stashed in the annals of history, compels us to examine its hidden secrets and also makes us think of the possibility of ancient worlds taking a trip right into the icy core of Antarctica.

A very extensive piece of cartography that was developed in the 16th century as well as passes the name of the Orontius Finaeus Map. It is also called the Orontius Finaeus Map. Orontius Finaeus, that was a mathematician, astronomer, as well as cartographer in France, was the one who created it. The portrayal of Antarctica on this map establishes it as unique from other maps of the moment because, according to the accepted version of history, Antarctica was not supposed to be discovered for many more centuries.

When Orontius Finaeus developed his map in 1531, the age of the Antarctic expedition was still many centuries away from the beginning. The usually accepted account sets the exploration of Antarctica somewhere in the very early 19th century, with travellers such as James Cook as well as Fabian Gottlieb von Bellingshausen laying case to the honour of being the initial to find the continent. Despite this, the Orontius Finaeus Map portrays Antarctica, as full of mountains, coastlines, as well as rivers. The map was created by the Greek cartographer Orontius.

Several implications could be obtained from such a very early portrayal of Antarctica. It is feasible that Orontius Finaeus had access to old maps or other resources that revealed the mysteries of this frozen continent. Or is there an additional, more ordinary factor for this cartographic peculiarity that we have overlooked?

According to one college of thought, the Orontius Finaeus Map may have been derived from older maps or expertise that had been handed down via the generations. The proponents of this hypothesis contend that old seafarers, who lived before the typical European travellers, might have sailed into the waters of Antarctica, where they might have left graphs and papers that were later utilized by cartographers like Orontius Finaeus.

Orontius Finaeus might have employed a different kind of map projection, which might have distorted Antarctica's topography, providing the perception that it lay better to the north than it was. This is one of the theories that is produced in an additional proposition. According to this interpretation, the map does not show an authentic early expertise of Antarctica; instead, it demonstrates a cartographic error.

On the other hand, the Orontius Finaeus Map additionally has some enticing features that add to the ongoing conversation over old travel. It has a canal that is known as the "Sinus Magnus," as well as it is extremely similar to the Ross Sea, which is a significant entry of the Antarctic shoreline. This function might be discovered in this world. On top of that, there are depictions of mountains and rivers on the map, which leads one to question the beginnings of such geographical knowledge.

The enigma becomes extra complex when we take into factor to consider the map's apparent expertise of ice-free areas within Antarctica. It details areas of the continent that, in conformity with contemporary understanding, must in point of reality have been without ice during previous times in the background of the world. Is it feasible that this is a representation of the information that was given using past civilizations that formerly prospered in distinct weather conditions?

In the look for answers, the Map of Orontius Finaeus has been the focus of clinical investigation and close examination. Some professionals contend that the portrayal of Antarctica on the map may mirror geographical features that existed during earlier dates, maybe also in the distant past when they were devoid of ice cover. They imply that Orontius Finaeus may have compiled his map making use of details gleaned from a selection of resources, such as old manuscripts as well as charts.

Nevertheless, many believe that the representation of Antarctica on the map could be the product of several aspects, including mistakes in the map's projection, opinion, as well as the extrapolation of geographical details from minority resources available at the time. They argue that the map does not always reveal a firsthand understanding of the genuine topography of Antarctica which is their major debate.

The Orontius Finaeus Map, with its complex mix of location, background, and guesswork, urges us to contemplate the nature of exactly how details are given from generation to generation through background. It compels us to participate in important considering the information sources that have added to the building and construction of our understanding of the globe, along with the function that cartography plays in the upkeep as well as dissemination of that expertise.

The Orontius Finaeus Map functions as a prompt tip that the restrictions of human understanding are not static but rather continuously broadening as we discover ourselves at a crossroads where academia and the unknown satisfy. It encourages us to explore the possibility of long-lost worlds and the possibility of information that has been concealed, both of which can eventually reword the background of discovery.

Join me, dear viewers, as we triggered on an experience right into the realm of the Orontius Finaeus Map to decode the secrets it reveals as well as the secrets it conceals concerning the limits of human query as well as understanding. It is a voyage that motivates us to ponder on the ever-present fascination of the obscure and also the relentless wish for details that thrust us onward via the halls of history.

CHAPTER 21:
ONGOING RESEARCH
STUDY AS WELL
AS DISCUSSIONS
" UNSOLVED
ARTEFACTS TODAY."

Certain secrets continue to stand up to the unstoppable onward motion of time, as well as particular loosened threads continue to be a tantalising component of the ever-changing tapestry that is human background. These are the mysteries surrounding old artefacts, the remains of past eras that remain to provide obstacles to our understanding and also evoke warm conflicts amongst academics, fans, and excavators. Old artefacts remain to fascinate and frustrate people long after they were initially discovered, and as we go onward into the current day, we find ourselves amid a landscape of active research study and intriguing puzzles.

The Antikythera Mechanism is an example of such an artefact that continues to baffle and fascinate its audiences. The difficult gadget that is commonly referred to as the globe's initial analogue computer system was discovered in the wreckage of a ship that came from the Roman period in 1901 off the coast of the island of Antikythera, which is situated in Greece. It consists of several pieces of equipment as well as dials that have been meticulously constructed to an amazing level of accuracy.

The function of the Antikythera Device is still an issue that is being extensively investigated as well as talked about. Some people think it was utilized to calculate astronomical occurrences, while others say it was used for navigation or perhaps as an educational tool. Still, others think it was used to calculate huge events. Our ability to comprehend the depth of scientific information held by the ancient Greeks is extended to its limitations by the intricacy and technical skill of this artefact.

Scientists actually could take a look at the inner functions of the Antikythera Mechanism through the usage of sophisticated imaging approaches such as X-rays as well as three-dimensional tomography over the program of several years. Through these analyses, more degrees of ins and outs and sophistication have been discovered, which has assisted in drawing light on the possible roles as well as objectives. There are still a lot of concerns that haven't been attended to, as well as the equipment has maintained its air of mystery, which proceeds to record people's imaginations.

The Voynich Manuscript is yet an additional artefact that is presently at the centre of questions and controversy that is still continuous. This mystical publication was founded in 1912 by unusual bookseller Wilfrid Voynich. It is written in a script that nobody is familiar with and loaded with elegant photos of greenery, human beings, and expensive events. The text has not been decrypted regardless of the efforts of numerous scientists and cryptographers collaborating.

Codebreakers have been damaging their heads for generations over the Voynich Manuscript. Its manuscript, which is unlike any kind of other creating system understood, develops an overwhelming obstacle to analyzing the components of the paper. Others think it may be a sophisticated fraud or a made-up language, while others think it may be a kind of cypher or code. Still, others believe it may be a smart fake.

It's intriguing to keep in mind that the drawings in the publication are equally as puzzling as the text itself. The plants that are represented on its web pages do not correlate to any type of acknowledged species, and also the appearance of what seems womanly beings floating in a fluid provides the guide's pages with a surrealist top quality. The function of the manuscript, its beginnings, and also the identity of the individual who composed it are all an enigma to this particular day, which aids to make it one of the enigmas that have continued the lengthiest in the composed world.

One more artefact that proceeds to feed disputes and ignite people's interest is called the Baghdad Battery. This thing was located amongst the ruins of Khujut Rabu, which is located near Baghdad in Iraq. It consists of 3 various parts: a clay container, a copper cylinder, and an iron rod. Among the most fascinating facets of the exploration is the opportunity that the item in the inquiry was an old battery that was able to produce a very small quantity of electrical fee.

The theory that the Baghdad Battery might have been used for electroplating or other kinds of electrochemical operations raises problems concerning the amount of scientific understanding that was held by old human beings. Also while some specialists have recommended alternate interpretations, such as the container being absolutely nothing greater than a storage vessel, the enigma of the Baghdad Battery remains to captivate us and also urges us to consider the methods in which ancient modern technology might have been used.

The Lycurgus Cup is yet one more artefact that extends the boundaries between the fields of art and science. It has mesmerising high qualities, which have captivated scholars. This Roman glass goblet, which dates back to the 4th century CE, is well-known for the fact that its colour can change from one colour to one more. It creates a sight that runs out of this globe when lit from behind, altering from environment-friendly to red as it does so.

Via making use of contemporary spectroscopic investigation, the mystery of the Lycurgus Mug's chameleon-like ability to change colour was solved. It was uncovered that the glass includes extremely tiny nanoparticles of silver and gold, which, when revealed to light, cause a spectacular modification in colour. It is not recognized for sure what the goblet was used for or how significant it remained in old Rome; nonetheless, some individuals think that it may have been utilized in rituals or wonderful practices at the time.

Stone Spheres of Costa Rica is a yet more mysterious team of artefacts that continue to dumbfound scholars and excavators today. These enormous rock rounds may be discovered dispersed around the Diquis Delta in the southern region of Costa Rica. Their diameters range from just a couple of inches to several feet. These balls are famous for the near-perfect geometric perfection that they possess, as well as they are sculpted from diorite and granite.

The Stone Spheres have remained a secret, both in regards to their function as well as their history. Some theories suggest that they might have acted as pens for calendrical or astronomical events, while others hypothesize that they may have played a substantial role in ceremonies or routines. Their extraordinary skill, accomplished without using any type of device made from steel, resists our perceptions of the powers of ancient rock carvers.

The enigmas that surround the Baghdad Battery, the Lycurgus Mug, as well as the Rock Spheres of Costa Rica offer a tip that, also in our contemporary globe, there are still lots of keys to be fixed.

Even in this day and age, with all the advances in modern technology and research study that has been done, the past still has specific secrets that defy basic explanations. These artefacts encourage us to review the degree of a class of old people and also the methods by which their knowledge might be put into contemporary troubles.

As we make our method with the labyrinth of constant research and discussion that borders these mysteries that have not been answered, we are forced to face the ever-present appeal of the unidentified. Academics and researchers are required to be persons to address the problems that each artefact supplies, which are secrets that are just waiting to be revealed. We behold the complexity of human background as well as the endless opportunity for discovery that remains to urge us ahead in these artefacts.

Join me, dear visitor, as we set off on a voyage right into the mystical world of unusual artefacts in today's globe, a place where questions remain to exist, discussions grow, as well as the look for expertise remains to be an ever-changing as well as continuous effort. It is a trip that urges us to welcome the secrets of the past as well as the guarantee of future disclosures as we attempt to uncover the tricks of these ancient enigmas, and this invitation is available in the form of a voyage that prompts us to accept the mysteries of the past.

CHAPTER 22: THE STONEHENGE ENIGMA: EXISTS LASTLY A RESPONSE TO THIS MEGALITHIC PUZZLE?

Stonehenge, a primitive structure considered to be one of the most recognisable and mystical sites worldwide, lies in the bucolic setting of England's Salisbury Plain. This primitive work of art, which is made up of significant megalithic stones, has given intrigue and awe for ages, and it continues to resist easy explanation in this day and age. As we explore the riddles bordering Stonehenge, we discover that we are drawn better and deeper into a complicated maze that checks our understanding of ancient design, astronomy, and also society.

The mystery bordering Stonehenge may be mapped back over several centuries. The framework is qualified by its imposing rocks, large trilithons, as well as round design. It is approximated to have been produced in periods lasting from 3100 BCE to 1600 BCE. Because of the large size and precision engineering of the structure, the old people who built it posed serious issues regarding their abilities as well as the reasons behind their activities.

Concerning Stonehenge's feature has been, and also will certainly continue to be, among the most bewildering enigmas. Throughout centuries, a variety of hypotheses have been set up, varying from the building's use as a location of worship as well as ceremonial activities to that of a huge observatory and also a centre for recovery. Each of these theories weaves an extra layer right into the detailed fabric of the likely definitions behind Stonehenge.

Stonehenge may have been utilized as an astronomical observatory, with its positioning being calculated according to the motions of several celestial bodies, according to one prominent concept. The placement of the monument with the solstices, and also in particular the summertime solstice, has been a central subject of discussion regarding this idea. At the time of the summer solstice, the rising sun and the Heel Stone remain in best alignment with one another, which enables a shaft of light to penetrate the centre of the rock circle.

Many people assume that Stonehenge was used to track the solar schedule and to honour substantial farming or spiritual events attached to the modification of the seasons due to its alignment with the celestial spheres. The challenging design of the monument as well as its use of megalithic developments indicate that its developers had a profound understanding of the physics of the cosmos.

There is some conjecture that Stonehenge was used as a cemetery at some point in its background. The discovery of cremated human remains during excavations performed within and also around the monolith has motivated some individuals to hypothesise that it served either as a cemetery or a location of memory for the ancient aristocracy. Nonetheless, the level to which these burial places are connected to the overarching function of Stonehenge is still a matter of some contention.

Researchers have also been baffled by the building strategies that were made use of to develop Stonehenge. It is vague exactly how the huge stones, some of which evaluate approximately 50 tonnes each, were relocated and placed, which elevates uncertainties about the design proficiency and organisational abilities of the people who built them. It has been hypothesised that sledges, wooden rollers, and human labour were made use of in the process of relocating and raising the stones; however, the details of this process remain the subject of examination and testing.

Over the last few years, experts actually could discover covert elements below the surface of the Stonehenge landscape many thanks to the application of sophisticated modern technology such as ground-penetrating radar and also three-dimensional laser scanning. Our understanding of the value of the site has come to be much more nuanced as a result of these searchings, which include burial mounds, rock circles, and paths that were not previously recognised.

Stonehenge is not an isolated monument but rather an element of a larger complicated of historic locations and features, including. Stonehenge's background and function are intricately linked, and the adjoining avenue, the Cursus, and the bluestone quarry in Wales, which donated a few of the rocks, all add their one-of-a-kind method to this internet.

The inquiry of who created Stonehenge is most likely one of the mysteries that will certainly remain unresolved for the foreseeable future. Although it is typically thought that the Druids or the Celts are responsible for the creation of the monument, its timeframe of building predates the videotaped historical visibility of any one of these teams. A recent research study exposes that the building contractors might have been a varied community of individuals, consisting of those from far locations that collected on Salisbury Level to build this magnificent structure. These people may have taken a trip from a country mile to deal with this job.

We are brought in person with the remarkable web link that exists between the past and the existing when we are challenged by the enormous stones that make up Stonehenge. The monument compels us to reassess our preconditioned ideas of past people, the expertise they had, and the objectives that drove them. It urges us to value the tricks that have continued throughout the background in addition to the infinite possibility for discovery that hinges on shop for us in this day and age.

Join me, my visitor, as we proceed our trip deeper right into the centre of the enigma bordering Stonehenge. We will examine the questions that continue to be asked and also the continuous study that remains to peel back the layers of this old-time problem. This is a trip that urges us to approve the difficulty of our common human past and to express joy in the attraction of the mystical that has lingered throughout the ages.

CHAPTER 23: STONEHENGE: DIGGING UP THE HIDDEN TRUTHS BEHIND IT

Stonehenge is shrouded in a myriad of secrets, both unnoticeable and noticeable to the naked eye. As we continue to check out the strange world of this ancient monolith, we currently change our emphasis to the proceeding excavations and explorations that have the perspective to toss brand-new light on the mysteries that lie concealed under the adored ground of Salisbury Level.

Excavators have gotten an objective in the last few years to discover the keys that lie concealed under the surface of Stonehenge. Outfitted with cutting-edge devices and also new research study methods, these archaeologists have gone on their journey. Due to their efforts, a complex landscape of old attributes, frameworks, as well as artefacts has been revealed, as well as our expertise in this well-known area has been rethought.

The finding of secret stone circles all over the key monument is just one of the most significant searchings that has been made. Archaeologists have found proof of stone circles that were formerly unidentified to them by using ground-penetrating radar as well as aerial surveys. A few of these stone circles go back to the same time duration as the primary monolith. Even though they are much smaller in size than Stonehenge's other circles, the information that can be amassed from these circles on the bigger Stonehenge ritualistic and routine landscape is incredibly helpful.

One of these was a gigantic rock circle referred to as "Superhenge," which was discovered around 3 kilometres away from the key site. Our conception of Stonehenge as a solitary structure is cast doubt by the visibility of this circle, which comprises at the very least 90 standing rocks and has a circumference of more than 100 metres. The presence of Superhenge offers proof that the surrounding region was soon a dynamic centre of ancient tasks, with several stone circles located around the area meeting a selection of huge or ceremonial features.

The link between Stonehenge and the landscape that surrounds it has likewise come into clearer light as an outcome of this. Current research has shown that there is a network of paths, frequently understood as "processional ways," that connect Stonehenge to surrounding monuments like the Cursus, which is a huge earthwork enclosure. These sidewalks provide the perception that Stonehenge was not only a static monument but rather a dynamic part of broader ceremonial tasks or routines that happened around the surrounding location.

Stonehenge as well as the bordering area have been dug deep into thoroughly, which has resulted in the exploration of a riches of artefacts and also information. Locates consist of melted human remains, animal bones, as well as ritualistic artefacts, all of which offer fascinating hints regarding the rites and events that took place on the website. The presence of these artefacts offers support to the theory that the architects as well as customers of Stonehenge affixed a substantial amount of social and spiritual importance to the framework.

A subterranean network of caverns and tunnels has been located beneath Stonehenge, which is among the most fascinating explorations that have been made. Utilizing ground-penetrating radar as well as laser scanning, subterranean frameworks have been revealed. These features consist of a large funeral pile referred to as the "Superhenge lengthy barrow" and also a collection of openings called the "Aubrey Holes." Beneath the recognisable rocks might exist a rich layering of rites, funeral services, and various other activities, as shown by these underground attributes.

The feature of the Aubrey Holes, which have been known concerning considering that the moment of John Aubrey, an antiquarian who resided in the 17th century and discovered them for the very first time, is still unidentified. Some professionals think that they functioned as markers for expensive events, while others think that they might have brought wood messages or rocks. Both of these theories have obtained assistance from other researchers. The fact that even more Aubrey Holes have been discovered recently, bringing the overall variety of openings in the known circle up from 56 to 66, has added to the secret.

As we proceed to check out better into the underground enigmas of Stonehenge, we are consulted with an extensive understanding of our oneness with everything around us. The monument, which was initially considered a single structure, is now seen to be a component of a higher landscape that is rich in the importance of rituals and events. The individuals that developed it were not separated by any means; instead, they were a component of a culture that was ever-changing and vibrant, as well as they left their imprint on the landscape in a variety of different methods.

The continuous studies as well as excavations at Stonehenge act as a reminder that background is not a static story but instead a living puzzle that continues to develop through time. The strange attraction of the monument remains to enthral us, and also it has motivated fresh generations of academics and travellers to uncover the mysteries that are still concealed underneath its old-time rocks.

Join me, dear visitor, as we check out the ongoing excavations and discoveries that promise to transform our expertise in this olden mystery as we go even further. This is a trip that encourages us to recognise the continuing pressure of inquisitiveness in addition to the endless opportunities for exploration that the ancient world still has.

CHAPTER 24: A VANISHED HUMAN BEING HID DEEP WITHIN THE EARTH: GÖBEKLI TEPE

There is a site in the centre of southeastern Turkey that resists the standard chronicles of human background. It is situated in the undulating landscape of the historic area of Anatolia, which is home to the Anatolian Plateau. Göbekli Tepe, which equates to "Potbelly Hill" in English, shows up before us like a guard from the midsts of antiquity, urging us to peel back the layers of the past and also expose a failed to remember world lying below the dirt.

The history of Göbekli Tepe began in the 1960s when a team of archaeologists led by Klaus Schmidt discovered the site and exposed its presence to the general public for the extremely very first time. What they uncovered was nothing short of astounding; it was a big historical facility that dated back to about 9600 BCE, making it one of the earliest well-known buildings that was set up by human hands.

The amazing rock columns at Göbekli Tepe, which act as guards of the past, go to the centre of the enigma bordering this ancient website. These columns, a few of which are over 5 metres tall as well as considered numerous tonnes, are not straightforward monoliths but rather elegant items of art. There is a menagerie of animals, including distressing lions, nimble boars, and also sophisticated birds, every one of which was given birth to by the gifted hands of old musicians and sculpted onto the surfaces of these items.

These carvings have greater than simply a visual purpose; rather, they are deeply considerable from a symbolic and ritualistic point of view. They provide a home window into the cosmological and spiritual concepts of individuals who created Göbekli Tepe as well as saw it often. Each pillar associates a tale, one that concentrates as well as covers the centuries on the connection that exists between people and the all-natural world.

The lack of evidence for permanent occupancy at Göbekli Tepe is just one of the characteristics that set it apart from other old websites. There are no residences, fireplaces, or other indicators of household life to be located. Rather, it appears as though the area functioned as a focal point for societal meetings, events, and possibly also huge observations. Its function is to be located in the domain name of the holy, at the crossway of the beautiful realm and the old globe.

The building style of Göbekli Tepe is another among the historical wonders that can be seen there. The place has numerous concentric units, which are sometimes described as "temples," and each of these "temples" includes its very own collection of massive stone columns put in a rounded pattern. These enclosures were developed throughout the program time, with later ones frequently being improved on top of earlier ones deliberately. This created a strata of background that is presently waiting to be uncovered.

The rooms of Göbekli Tepe are arranged in a circular pattern, providing the website the feel of a sanctuary, as well as there are stone pillars that emit out from the centre. It is a monument to the intricacy of its designers, who had a deep grasp of geometry, layout, as well as the symbolic relevance of circular spaces. This is evidenced by the fact that it is a circular structure.

The huge facet of the stone columns triggers one to contemplate the constructability of the framework all at once. The fact that the old people who developed Göbekli Tepe could not collaborate with metal devices, as well as the wheel, makes the accomplishment even more impressive. The exact procedures that were employed to cut, transport, as well as increase these huge stones are still being researched and also gone over today.

The methodical burying of Göbekli Tepe's rooms over the training course of time is perhaps one of the most remarkable characteristics of this old site. while fresh cages were developed, the previous ones were actively buried under layers of soil as well as garbage while the building of newer ones proceeded. This burial ceremony gives a glimpse right into an advanced belief system in addition to an awareness of the repeated patterns that underlie rejuvenation, fatality, and life.

As we review Göbekli Tepe's feature within the larger structure of human history, the enigma bordering this site just grows much deeper. It casts questions on the standard account, which specifies that the development of intricate human beings can be traced back to the appearance of farming and the cleared-up way of life. Instead, it suggests that the drive for community conferences, rituals, and the building of big frameworks precedes the practice of well-established farming, which presses back the duration of the formation of human culture and also technical advancement.

As we continue to discover the realm of Göbekli Tepe, we are advised that background is not a collection of events that happened in sequential order but rather a tapestry of intertwined stories that are simply waiting to be discovered. The constant excavation as well as studies at the website are expected to introduce extra levels of complication and enigma, which will certainly invite us to reassess what we know about old human beings and the deep means by which people have communicated with their setting and also their beliefs.

Join me, dear visitor, as we go even more into the lost globe under the soil and also explore the continuous excavations and explorations that remain to transform our understanding of Göbekli Tepe. Göbekli Tepe is a place where the past comes to life and also the mysteries of classical times welcome us to explore the midsts of their mysteries. It is a voyage that extends an invitation to us to link with our old forefathers and to welcome the everlasting allure of the mystical prizes that continue to await their discovery hidden below the sands of time.

CHAPTER 25: THE EXPENSIVE SIGNIFICANCE OF GÖBEKLI TEPE

As we dive much more into the complex puzzle of Göbekli Tepe, our investigation leads us to contemplate the tremendous planetary link that the location has with the cosmos. Göbekli Tepe pleads us to consider its function as a bridge between the earthly and heavenly worlds, where ancient peoples looked at the skies with wonder and also respect. Beneath the layers of earth and also time, Göbekli Tepe bids us to analyze its duty as a bridge between the earthly and holy realms.

The Göbekli Tepe stone pillars, which are covered with complicated makings of pets as well as symbolic patterns, tell a story that exceeds the realm of the earthly world. Countless experts are of the point of view that these engravings have some type of link to the paradises; they are claimed to symbolize the constellations, celebrities, as well as various other astronomical phenomena that the ancient individuals who built this website adored and enjoyed.

The possibility that Göbekli Tepe was previously used as an ancient observatory is just one of the most interesting ideas worrying the site. The positioning of the stone columns in circular enclosures, with the columns regularly guided towards a particular position on the perspective, hints at a deliberate connection with huge incidents. Some academics think that astronomical measurements were executed at Göbekli Tepe and that these monitorings were used to note considerable holy incidents like the solstices and also equinoxes.

The astronomical analysis is provided extra support by the sculptures that are on the rock columns. Among the portrayals of animals, numerous monsters especially stand out as feasible personifications of constellations or various other beautiful numbers. For example, the scorpion is shown on lots of pillars, and its presence might have some link to the constellation Scorpius. Several of the sculptures show birds in flight, which may be seen as an indicator of the heavenly realm.

The concept that Göbekli Tepe was linked to the heavens in some method is given more support by the means the monolith is outlined geographically. A clear view of the evening skies would certainly have been feasible due to the position of the structure, which was set down on top of a hillside and supplied a sweeping vista of the area around it. In old times, when there was no such point as artificial illumination, the evening skies would have been filled up with a lot more breathtaking canopy of stars.

The existence of the Marauder Rock at Göbekli Tepe is among the most persuading items of evidence that the website had some kind of huge significance. This substantial block, which evaluates many tonnes, is carved plainly with a representation of a marauder with its wings spread wide in trip. Some academics think that this marauder may be symbolic of a celestial bird or maybe an ancient famous character attached to the divine realms.

The concept that Göbekli Tepe was an observatory implied noting essential huge events is provided added credence by the reality that the positioning of the Marauder Rock within among the rooms accompanied the sunup of the winter months solstice. On the early morning of the winter solstice, the sun's rays would have lit the Marauder Stone. This would certainly have resulted in a magnificent interplay of light and shadow, which would have highlighted the value of the vulture.

The connection to the heavens that was uncovered at Göbekli Tepe elevates some essential problems about the beliefs as well as worldviews of the old people who developed it. They sought to map the skies to obtain a far better understanding of the cosmos. Did they perceive the divine world as a source of divine inspiration? The sculptures as well as the positionings at the site give the perception that there was an advanced interaction between spirituality, culture, and astronomy.

The truth that Göbekli Tepe is attached to the universe obliges us to consider where it fits into the higher scope of the history of ancient people. Could it be that Göbekli Tepe shows the start of mankind's endless obsession with the paradises and the points that take place in them? It calls right into inquiry our preconditioned concepts about the development of astronomy as well as the search for solutions to the mysteries of the cosmos if this is the case.

As we continue to introduce the secrets of Göbekli Tepe, we are reminded that the website is not just a remnant of the past but instead a portal to a world where the earthly and holy globes clashed. This realisation works as a pointer that Göbekli Tepe is greater than simply an antique of the past. It is a location where ancient peoples sought the paradises as well as left behind a record of their awe and respect for the cosmological mysteries that were throughout them.

Allow us not to fail to remember that it is a trip that asks us to connect the gap between the earthly and the incredible, in addition, to honour the continuous heritage of those who aim to reach out and touch celebrities.

CHAPTER 26: THE MYSTERIES THAT HAVE PERSISTED WITH TIME IN ANCIENT ARTEFACTS

We locate ourselves at the tail end of history, in the centre of the ruins as well as residues of the old globe, poised on the verge of understanding and amazement. This examination right into the puzzles of ancient artefacts has been a voyage with the web pages of a tapestry that has been woven with threads of revelation, enigma, as well as mystery. This journey has unravelled like a trip with a tapestry. However, as our trip involves an end, we are advised that the secrets of the previous remain to captivate us to this particular day, as well as that their charm has not been dulled by the relentless march of time.

Throughout the program of our journey, we have explored the midsts of time in an initiative to decipher the enigmas that are entombed inside the real material of historic antiques. The Antikythera System is a work of art of old design that resists our preconditioned presumptions of what makes up high-level scientific skill, as well and we have discovered its most mysterious depths. We have now gone into the strange realm of the Voynich

Manuscript, a mystical cypher that is still past our ability to analyze. We have examined the mystery bordering the Baghdad Battery, which is a testimony to the opportunity that electricity was harnessed in old times.

The Lycurgus Mug, with its mesmerising color-changing high qualities, has astounded our detects and also welcomed us to discover the communication of art as well as science in antiquity. These features are in charge of the mug's capacity to transform colours. The Stone Balls of Costa Rica, which serve as peaceful sentinels amid exotic rain forests, have piqued our passion for the long-vanished human beings that soon populated these lands and also formed the landscapes we see today.

Stonehenge, which has been there for a long time and also has become an enduring symbol of old Britain, has always functioned as a demonstration of the endless powers of human architecture as well as creative thinking. Recent excavations have exposed a complicated landscape composed of stone circles, processional paths, and also underground secrets, which has compelled us to review what we assumed we understood regarding this mysterious monolith.

Furthermore, when we discover the tricks of the Piri Reis Map as well as the Orontius Finaeus Map, we are advised to analyze the limitations of old understanding in addition to the possibilities of vanished civilizations that cruised the undiscovered waters of discovery.

These artefacts, each of which stands for a chapter in the annals of human background, function as a tip that the past is not a shut book but rather an ever-evolving story. Each brand-new discovery functions as a page flip, and each enigma presents a new task to be addressed. They motivate us to accept the mysterious, to cherish the mystery of the unknown, and also to commemorate the everlasting force of human questions and exploration by promoting these things.

The reality that ancient artefacts proceed to confound contemporary scientists despite the flow of time is proof that wonder can endure the onslaught of time. They act as a pointer that even in this day as well as age of advanced technology and clinical investigation, the past is still a labyrinthine world filled with mysteries that are asking to be unravelled as well as concerns that have yet to be dealt with.

As we reach the completion of our investigation right into the enigmas bordering old artefacts, we are filled with a remarkable feeling of wonder as well as humbleness. Old artefacts are not just antiques; rather, they stand for home windows into the infinite human yearning for connection, imagination, as well as comprehension. They work as a poignant reminder that the past is not some distant location, but rather a background that most of us share, a tapestry that is woven with the threads of plenty of generations.

As a component of our pursuit of understanding, we have been charged with acting both as travellers and as guardians of the past; we are responsible for maintaining its valuable artefacts and illuminating its perplexing secrets. The unresolved challenges offer us chances to function together, put our creativity to the examination, and expand our admiration for the phenomenal accomplishments of those who came before us. Every one of these things is essential for moving on.

In this method, when we state our farewells to the secrets of ancient artefacts, we take with us the unquenchable curiosity that has been the driving pressure behind our tour. It is feasible that we may never have the ability to decode every one of the secrets of the past; nevertheless, the search for expertise, much like the artefacts themselves, is a trip that transcends both time and generations.

When we say farewell to the artefacts that have enlightened us regarding their secrets, we do it with a feeling of recognition and wonder, along with the understanding that the adventure of discovery will proceed, ever onward, right into the obscure frontiers of human history.

I would certainly intend to reveal my gratitude to you, my dear readers, for accompanying me on my journey to find ancient artefacts. I want you that the unsolved challenges of the past will certainly remain to enthral your imagination and encourage your pursuit of understanding.

ABOUT THE AUTHOR

Rup Rani

Author Rup Rani is well-known for her fascinating fiction and useful nonfiction. She has a deep-seated need to inform tales, as well as she does so by crafting moving narratives that reverberate with her audience. Rup's writing is mentally felt by visitors throughout the globe because of her capability to masterfully integrate personal experience with substantial research.

Rup's love of books sprang from his normally dazzling imagination as well as his curious nature. She invested her youth in a little village reading to get away from reality as well as into the enchanted worlds crafted by authors that stimulated her creative imagination. Rup's coming-of-age years accompanied the time when she found her very own unique voice and also learned to reveal the deep need she had actually constantly had to make stories revive and also share them with others.

Rup's composing style is a magnificent synthesis of reflective representation as well as a cautious research study. Her dedication to honesty, as well as precise research study, are evident in her writing, leaving a long-lasting impression on her visitors. Rup infuses her tales with real compassion and relatability by drawing on her individual experiences of failing, success, and self-discovery. Her creation makes her personalities real, and their experiences catch the richness of the human experience.

Rup Rani's posts are founded not simply on her very own

experiences but additionally on considerable study. She is a firm follower in diving into a variety of subjects in order to better recognize the globe as well as the individuals in it. Rup's commitment to exhaustive study and also her love of finding out produce works that contain understanding and also sparkle. Her nonfiction writing is highly concerned with its capacity to enlighten, inspire, and also change people's worldviews.

Rup Rani's flexibility and also aesthetic range get on screen in her capability to compose throughout styles. Her words have the prospective to take visitors to new worlds of creativity and knowledge, whether she is informing a heartbreaking tale of love and also loss or probing facility social motifs. Every syllable resounds with the creativity that she has put into her operation in an effort to push herself additionally than she has preceded.

Rup Rani's viewers have a unique affection for her as a writer. Her writing has been applauded by doubters and she has gotten a large fan base from viewers that react to her ability to make them feel something or make them believe. Rup really hopes that the tales she informs will have a long-lasting impact on her viewers, prompting them to examine their own lives and make conscious initiatives in the direction of improvement as well as knowledge.

Rup Rani's non-writing time is invested in appreciating the marvels of the environment, seeking her passion for photography, and also having thoughtful conversations with other innovative kinds. Her deep admiration permanently as well as pressing curiosity regarding the world around her offer powerful sources of ideas for her art.

Rup Rani's genuine storytelling and also insightful observations continue to sway readers with each succeeding magazine. She creates both fiction and also nonfiction with the purpose of motivating others to value language, to believe critically about their surroundings, as well as to set out on their own courses of personal growth.

Rup Rani's enthusiasm for creating, notified by her life experiences and scholastic research study, has made her a house name. Her works move visitors deeply, making them believe and also maybe inspiring them to do something about it. Rup Rani is still a literary giant, recording readers with her exceptional narrative abilities as well as unflinching devotion to realistic looks as she digs further and much deeper into the complexity of the human problem.

www.ingramcontent.com/pod-product-compliance
Lightning Source LLC
Chambersburg PA
CBHW050826260726
48660CB00004B/1635